The Success Factor

Dr Robert Sharpe is one of B[...] behavioural management of stress and anxiety. He has pioneered new methods of treatment for phobias and anxiety states, especially flying phobias. He has also researched stress in industry, marital and sexual problems, and the difficulties of examination students.

Through his London practice and his training institute, Dr Sharpe organises seminars and training workshops for social workers, psychiatrists, psychologists, teachers and nurses. He also lectures extensively to industrialists.

David Lewis has worked extensively as a journalist in England and Europe. In 1969 he became a director and editor of the international syndication service, Features International, which he left in 1973 to become a freelance writer. He is especially interested in the legal system and in techniques of subversion, and has written books on both these subjects.

Dr Robert Sharpe and David Lewis

The Success Factor

How to be who *you* want to be

Pan Books London and Sydney

First British edition published 1976 by Souvenir Press Ltd
This edition published 1977 by Pan Books Ltd,
Cavaye Place, London SW10 9PG
© Dr Robert Sharpe and David Lewis 1976
ISBN 0 330 25179 1
Printed and bound in Great Britain by
Hunt Barnard Printing Ltd, Aylesbury, Bucks

Contents

How to use this book

This is a book about change.

Change for the better in your life.

In it we shall teach you how to use the powerful principles of learning to obtain success and fulfilment.

The book is divided into six parts. Each part has been written according to the psychological principles which are being taught. It is important, therefore, to read the book in the order and at the speed which we dictate in the text.

Parts One to Four should be read and put into practice before you attempt to put into effect your own programme of change.

In Part Five we describe, in detail, twelve commonly expressed goals. These include programmes which help you pass examinations, gain advancement in your career, enjoy fulfilling sexual and marital relationships, deal effectively with children's difficulties, control weight problems, make new friends, speak in public, control stress whilst flying and driving and play a better game of golf. It is not necessary, although you may wish to do so out of interest, to read all of this part, but rather to select those areas which particularly relate to your own needs.

The skills and strategies taught in the twelve specific goals can be used as the basis for any other programme of success of your own. The ways in which this can be done will be explained in the introduction to this part of the book.

In Part Six we shall detail the Laws of Learning and the ways in which you can ensure that your new behaviour remains effective in the long-term.

The principles of behaviour change know no barriers of age, class, sex or culture. They can be learned and put to work for you in a remarkably short space of time.

For many people the ways in which they and others behave, and the reasons why they respond as they do to certain situations, are something of a mystery. Once you have read this book and mastered the methods of behavioural analysis and change, mystery will be replaced by mastery. You will become the controller of your own destiny rather than the victim of circumstance.

Part one

In the first part of this book we shall present a framework of
knowledge, about how and why people behave as they do, within
which you can begin to consider your own behaviour and goals
in a new way. We will explain how you can consider them not as
haphazard responses to the world around you, or the products of
deep-seated and uncontrollable unconscious processes, but as
the result of patterns of learning which you can monitor
and alter at will.

This part of the book may be read over any convenient period of
time, but we do suggest that you absorb these revolutionary
concepts, which place the control of your behaviour in your own
hands, before proceeding to the rest of the book.

How to be who *you* want to be

There are times when even the happiest and best adjusted of us would like to be someone else. When we wish we could behave differently and more effectively in a particular situation. Perhaps we want to feel a greater confidence when starting a new job or more at ease when walking into a room full of strangers. Maybe sex makes us feel anxious and inhibited when we would sooner be able to relax and enjoy it. Perhaps we want to play a competitive sport as well as a friend who never seems to be thrown off balance by an early bad start to his game; take an examination without suffering agonising stomach cramps; or attend an interview and be certain we will make the best possible impression.

It happens to everybody. We attempt to do something only to fail because we cannot respond in the right way. Because we behave inappropriately we are not the people we want to be under those particular circumstances.

The thirty-year-old woman who came to see us not long ago was a sad example of this 'inability to behave as you want to behave' problem. Her marriage was on the verge of collapse because of the furious rows she had with her husband. The tragic thing was that they were still in love: 'I cannot seem to show him how much I love him,' the woman complained. 'When I try to act affectionately the words do not come out sounding right. When I try to be helpful he complains that I am being interfering.'

A similar problem confronted a middle-aged businessman who was on the point of being sacked by his company because of his inability to get on with his colleagues and subordinates. In private life a tolerant and understanding man, he found it impossible to express his true feelings to those working under him: 'Perhaps I am over-critical, but when I try to praise them they seem to get suspicious. I start a discussion meaning to emphasise the worth-while things they have done but end up tearing them apart. I can see myself doing it but I cannot see how to stop myself doing it!'

A young mother complained that she found it impossible to deal quietly and fairly with her two children. She did not regard herself as a harsh person, but that was the way it sounded to her family and especially to her younger son: 'I am always comparing Mike with John. I know it isn't fair on him but I cannot seem to help it. The remarks just slip out. I try to stay calm and tell them how much I really love them but I often end up losing my temper.'

Finally let us look at the case of an eighteen-year-old student who failed an important set of examinations. 'I knew my subject but when I came to take the papers I was so nervous I could not concentrate. I lost every scrap of confidence almost at once and knew I would fail.'

Often when confronted by this sort of situation we ask ourselves in exasperation – 'Why on earth did I behave like that?'

Sometimes we can see where we went wrong and know how we would like to behave. But understanding the problem is not enough. Insight into our difficulties *is* an essential starting point for change but it is not sufficient to effect that change *in the long-term*.

This qualification is very important. By really trying, an over-weight person may be able to stay on a diet long enough to shed several stone. By exerting every effort a heavy smoker should at least be able to reduce the number of cigarettes smoked per day. But the statistics for return to old habits in both these situations make depressing reading. One piece of research suggested that as many as ninety-seven per cent of would-be dieters had gone back to their former weight or even added a few pounds on top within twelve months of attempting to slim; while eighty-five per cent of heavy smokers returned to their old smoking habits within six months.

It is the same with more complex pieces of behaviour. A timid man may force himself to go to clubs and accept party invitations in the hope of making new friends. A shy and inhibited girl may try to behave like a passionate extrovert. But both will merely be acting out roles which they find uncomfortable and unnatural. They know *who* they want to be. Possibly they imagine themselves behaving with the ease and self-confidence of an envied friend or colleague. But the way they set about achieving their ambitions is incorrect and anxiety-producing. Inability to behave as you would like to behave can only be successfully overcome by eliminating inappropriate behaviours and replacing them with appropriate responses.

The main differences between a programme of behaviour modification, the subject of this book, and temporary adjustments are ease and permanence of change.

What is success?

We each have a different idea of what success means. It is a concept which alters many times during our lives. For the child at school it may mean being selected for a sports team or getting good grades. For the adolescent it may mean dating members of the opposite sex, forming deep friendships or finding an interesting career. The businessman may see success in terms of contracts, orders and promotions. The retired may seek success in creative activities for which there was never previously any spare time.

The definition used in the following programmes is a practical one, in that it can be put to work to attain any ambition.

Success=The setting up and attainment of goals

So far as this definition is concerned it is unimportant whether your goals are material or spiritual, social or sexual, long-term or short-term, simple or complex. They might be giving up smoking or losing weight, making friends more easily or enjoying a better sex life. You may want to study better or pass exams without stress, gain promotion or make the best possible impression at interviews. You may want to sleep more restfully, work more purposefully or play games more confidently. You may want to fly without fear or talk in public without tension.

Each of these goals, and an infinite number besides, is governed by our operational concept of success. Each and every one of them can be achieved by putting into practice the programmes for change described in this book.

These programmes are not a collection of social ploys nor a parade of one-upmanship tricks. We are not going to suggest you

13

tap a secret cosmic power, learn a form of mental gymnastics or exploit some hidden magic in your mind. What we will do is to explain and teach procedures of behavioural psychology which have, previously, been confined to the consulting rooms and clinics of professional therapists. They are procedures which have been perfected, during the last twenty-five years, in the world's psychological research laboratories. Under professional guidance they have helped millions of men and women to overcome problems and become the kind of people they really wanted to be.

Now we can show you how to employ these procedures on your own behalf: how to make scientifically founded principles of behaviour modification work for you. All it demands is a commitment of time and effort on your part, an investment in the present to change your future.

By studying and working at the programmes in this book you will learn how to accomplish the three key elements of successful change. First of all you will be shown how to analyse your life-style completely and accurately. You will discover the psychological and physiological reasons why you behave as you do: self-knowledge that provides the firm foundation on which new behaviours can be constructed. We will then show you how to expand your choice of alternatives so that you can identify the most effective and satisfying potential goals in your life.

Finally we will explain how you can programme your potential so that inappropriate behaviours are removed, and appropriate, goal-fulfilling responses put in their place, by the structured use of learning processes.

At this point you may be thinking: 'This is all very well, but surely we are as we are! Just as a person is born tall or short, fat or thin, blue-eyed or brown-eyed, so with behaviour. One individual is born confident, another retiring, one man bright, another man dim.'

Research has shown only vague justification for this fatalistic viewpoint. We are all born with a wide spectrum of potential. The tone-deaf may never be able to become concert pianists any more than most of us could aspire to change the course of physics as Einstein did. What we are concerned with is travelling as far as our potential ability will take us. We are concerned with freeing ourselves from the bondage of behaviours which did not arrive with our mother's milk; which were not written into our genetic programme; and which are present in our behavioural repertoire only because we have put them there. We have learned them through interactions with our environment.

This idea of *behaviour* as something learned may be a new one to you. In everyday language we tend to limit the use of the word. We talk of somebody being 'on their best behaviour' and of 're-volting behaviour' as though the concept embraced only an atten-tion to or a disregard for the particular manners and customs of our culture. In behavioural psychology behaviour has a clear definition: **behaviour is a response or set of responses made in a particular situation.**

The key words here are 'particular situation' because it is essen-tial to understand that behaviour can only usefully be considered in relation to the surroundings in which it takes place. To describe somebody as being 'very intolerant' or 'lacking in confidence' provides no real clue to their overall behaviour. A person who lacks confidence when meeting strangers may be capable of sailing alone around the world! Somebody who is intolerant of his chil-dren's mistakes may be the soul of patience when with a pretty woman.

The ways in which the environment influences behaviour is described as *stimulus control*. People behave as they do mainly because they come under stimulus control from their surround-ings. An example of this is the Jekyll and Hyde nature of some motorists. A person who is normally mild-mannered can turn into an aggressive lunatic behind the steering wheel. In a less dramatic way we respond to our surroundings at every waking moment. Food is generally a stimulus control to eat, orders from a superior exert a stimulus control to obey, soft music and dim lights a stimulus control to become romantic. Frequently the control exerted is so subtle that we are unaware of it, as in the case of a student who found himself unable to concentrate when studying for an examination. He complained that his attention wandered and he found himself reading the same page over and over again. An analysis of his studying behaviour revealed that he always worked with a stack of reference books on his desk. It was this

15

daunting mountain of material waiting to be absorbed that was preventing him from working effectively. Confronted with the physical evidence of so much labour ahead his confidence flagged. The books were exerting a *negative* stimulus control over his studying behaviour. The solution was to return all but two essential reference books to the shelves. With the stimulus control removed he was again able to study satisfactorily.

An even less obvious example of negative stimulus control was the case of a middle-aged woman who always felt nervous and unhappy when visiting her daughter-in-law. Because of this tension they had frequent rows. The problem was traced to a large and friendly cat owned by her son. The woman, although she had never realised it before, was mildly phobic of cats. Being confined in a small flat with a large animal was making her physically tense.

But our environments can just as easily exert a *positive* stimulus control on our behaviour. It is a matter of common observation that a fine day makes us feel happier and more energetic than a cold, wet miserable morning. A cheerful friend is more congenial company than a gloomy one. It is always more pleasant to receive a cheque than a bill! But, as with negative effects, these positive stimuli need not be so obvious. One male patient in his thirties complained of sexual difficulties with his wife. But it transpired that he also had a girl friend he saw only occasionally with whom he was able to enjoy satisfactory sex. In this case his wife was exerting a negative stimulus control over his sex drive, his girl friend a positive stimulus control.

One of the difficulties which insomniacs have is that, by lying awake in bed hour after hour, they come to associate bed not with sleep but with wakefulness. After a time they come under stimulus control to stay awake whenever they go to bed. Part of the cure is to break this stimulus control by making them get up and go into another room whenever they are unable to fall asleep within a predetermined time. This eventually removes the adverse stimulus control of the bed and bedroom.

We have mentioned the woman who was mildly phobic about cats and, of course, all phobics are excellent examples of people coming under stimulus control. In such cases a dog, an aircraft, open spaces or confined ones, spiders or snakes may all act as stimulus controls triggering a physical response that is often very violent.

But how does an environment come to exert this control in the first place? The answer is that we behave in a particular way in response to a certain stimulus because we have *learned* to do so.

In behavioural psychology *learning* is a very important process. We speak of learning to play an instrument or a game, to speak another language or drive a car. Less often appreciated is the fact that every single piece of behaviour in our repertoire – with the exception of reflex responses like the knee jerk – is there because we have *learned* it. We *learn* to show affection, to make love, to take examinations. If a person is able to compromise in negotiations, speak well in public or be at ease in social gatherings it is because he or she has *learned* to behave that way.

We appreciate that if we learn to play the piano or speak a language but do neither for several months our ability is going to decline. As the time passes we are not only getting rusty, we are also becoming less confident. The behaviour is going to become harder to perform and we are going to become increasingly reluctant to attempt it. The same rules apply to each and every other piece of behaviour which we have learned. In short, to virtually everything we do in life. If a man stops making love or talking to his partner about intimate feelings then both these important pieces of behaviour will become more difficult to carry out. If a person stops going out and meeting people then he will find it increasingly hard to do so. He will become less socially proficient and more and more reluctant to make the effort. We are not lonely, inhibited, under-confident or inarticulate through chance of birth or act of God but because we have learned to behave that way. We are not socially competent, confident and ambitious because of an inborn superiority but because we have learned such useful behaviours through fortunate interactions with our environment.

But why should such selective learning take place? What makes one piece of behaviour stick while another is forgotten? A piece of behaviour is learned if it is followed by a reward. Such rewards are called *reinforcers* and come in two kinds – *positive reinforcers* and *negative reinforcers*.

17

Research has shown that if a piece of behaviour is *immediately* followed by a reinforcer it is much more likely to be repeated than if that reinforcer is absent or if it is delayed.

A child helps with the washing up. The mother can offer her two kinds of rewards. The first is immediate praise. The second is a special treat in three days' time at the weekend. Which reinforcer is most likely to encourage the child to repeat the washing up behaviour?

The answer is the praise which comes directly after the behaviour even though it is less lavish than the distant reward. It is the speed rather than the magnitude of the reinforcer that is essential. This important point will be emphasised many times during the behaviour modification programmes in this book.

The more immediately a piece of behaviour is followed by a reinforcer the more effective will that reinforcer be in establishing that behaviour.

The greater the delay between a piece of behaviour and a reinforcer the less effective will that reinforcer be in establishing that behaviour.

This is one reason why people find it so hard to stick to a diet. Their reward, namely loss of weight, is never *immediate*, so that modification in eating behaviour is poorly established and depends on strength of purpose rather than actual behavioural change. In Part Five of the book we will outline a programme of weight control which overcomes this difficulty.

The concept of the *positive reinforcement* or the giving of a reward is easy to appreciate. We obtain such *positive reinforcement* when we win a prize, receive praise or acclaim, satisfy a hunger or experience some physical pleasure. Perhaps less readily understandable is the concept of the *negative reinforcer*. This is given when something unpleasant is removed from the situation following a piece of behaviour. This removal of discomfort or displeasure, for instance the tears of a child, the bad temper of a friend or the sarcasm of an employer, is equally effective in increasing the behaviour which immediately preceded it. For example a girl is looking miserable and her boyfriend kisses her.

As a result she smiles and appears happy. The boy has been *negatively reinforced* for his kissing behaviour. A child throws a tantrum and his mother comforts him. The bawling ceases. The mother has been *negatively reinforced* for her comforting behaviour.

But note also that the girl and the child have been *positively reinforced* for their pieces of behaviour. One was rewarded with a kiss the other with attention. In these interactions four kinds of learnings are being reinforced.

The girl is learning that looking miserable produces a reward (positive reinforcement).
The boy is learning that a kiss stops the girl being miserable (negative reinforcement).
The mother is learning that hugging her child stops him crying (negative reinforcement).
The child is learning that crying brings quick attention (positive reinforcement).

Incidentally there is a way out of this undesirable learning pattern which will be explained fully in Part Five of the book!

What would have happened if the girl, instead of smiling when she was kissed, had struck the boy sharply across the face? Suppose that the mother, rather than providing a warm body and soothing words, had smacked the child. Such punishing responses might have diminished those pieces of behaviour although it is by no means certain. A child seeking attention, for instance, may well feel that even a slap is better than maternal neglect. At the same time the side effects of such punishments could prove highly undesirable.

So far as the programmes in this book are concerned only rewarding situations will be used to establish new patterns of behaviour.

Finally let us look at a very common interaction in which response to one stimulus conditions your response to the next.

A man comes down to breakfast and finds an unexpected bill on his plate. It makes him irritable. He snaps at his wife and they row. He leaves for work in an angry frame of mind. Because of his temper he drives badly. He has a near accident and becomes extremely tense. By the time he arrives at the office he is in a very black mood. His colleagues reading the storm signals respond with anxiety or aggression. The man's digestion becomes upset. His head starts to ache. His brain, upset by feedback from his disturbed body, is unable to function efficiently. He makes mistakes. The mistakes make him even more irritable and nervous. At the end of such a day the man is likely to be exhausted and in no mood to appreciate his family or enjoy his night's rest.

We can probably all recognise days like his from our own experience. This man has suffered from a chain reaction called the 'halo effect'. One bad incident radiates a negative influence which becomes associated with the next situation. Because he has fared badly once he develops an expectancy that things will continue to go badly. This very anticipation of doom becomes a self-fulfilling prophecy. Emphasis tends to rest on unsatisfactory and unpleasant incidents while any oasis of pleasure is passed by.

The 'halo effect' is not necessarily negative. A bright start to the day, a piece of good news in the post, a cheerful smile or a general sense of well-being can just as easily set up a chain reaction of positive feeling. The important thing to realise is that when you are trapped by a negative 'halo effect' the apparently inevitable chain can be broken at any time by applying the correct behavioural cutting edge.

At this point you should prove to yourself that you have grasped the basic principles of behaviour which we have outlined, as a proper understanding is essential for the correct use of this book. Answer the following five questions by selecting one of the three suggested replies.

1 The effect on behaviour of a positive reinforcer is:
   (a) To increase it. (b) To decrease it. (c) Leave it unchanged.

2 For a positive or negative reinforcer to have the maximum effect it should come:
   (a) Just before the behaviour is carried out.
   (b) At the same time as the behaviour is carried out.
   (c) Just after the behaviour is carried out.

3 The effect of delaying a reinforcer long after the behaviour has been carried out is to:
(a) Strengthen its power. (b) Weaken its power.
(c) Leave it alone.

4 If a person is under stimulus control their behaviour is determined by:
(a) Factors in the environment.
(b) Childhood relationships.
(c) Their birth sign.

5 Negative reinforcement is the increase in a pattern of behaviour by:
(a) Punishing the person after behaviour.
(b) Removing a source of discomfort immediately after behaviour.
(c) Removing a source of discomfort immediately before behaviour.

If you have been able to answer these questions without referring to the text you are in a strong position to move on to the next part of the book. If you were uncertain about any of the terms then just re-read the explanations.

The second part of this book consists of a Fourteen-Day Programme designed to teach you the basic skills of behaviour modification and show you how to use them to change your own lifestyle in a small way.

But before you proceed with this programme we would like to stress the following points.

The lay-out of Parts Two and Three has been determined by the principles of behavioural psychology which are being taught. To succeed in its objectives of providing the skills and insights needed for effective change, this book requires two commitments on your part. First, it must be read in the order written and over the period of time stated in certain sections. Please do NOT skim, read ahead to find out what lies in store for you, nor move faster than the programme lays down even though you feel you have adequately grasped the points involved.

Secondly, the practical work must be carried out seriously or not at all. The procedures you will learn are not tricks or gimmicks but powerful instruments of behavioural change. They must either be used correctly on the basis of accurately collected data or they must be left alone.

This is a book not merely to be read but to be lived.

(Answers: 1a; 2c; 3b; 4a; 5b)

Part two

This will explain the ten skills needed to control and modify behaviour under any circumstances.

Fourteen-Day Programme

This section of the book must be read, day by day, over the two-week period for which it has been designed. The object of the programme is to enable you to put into practice, in a simple but effective way, the ten skills needed for behaviour change. You MUST follow the time-table as outlined, not being tempted to read ahead nor to proceed more quickly than the programme dictates. If you have a holiday or business trip planned which might interrupt the fourteen days, then we suggest you postpone the start of the training until there is an uninterrupted fortnight ahead. If you do miss a day or two it may be advisable to go back over some of the ground previously covered.

At the start of each day's programme we will list the approximate amount of time required for the exercises and the best times to carry them out. As a guide to aid you in pre-planning for the programme, it will never be necessary to devote more than sixty minutes per day to the exercises.

Introduction

Success = The setting up and attainment of goals

In order to put this definition into effect you must be able to carry out ten behavioural skills. These can be looked on as sub-goals or stepping stones on the way to attaining control over your lifestyle.

First of all we will explain what each skill entails then, during the Fourteen-Day Programme, you will put them into practice.

The ten skills for success comprise:

Sub-goal 1   Establishing an overall goal or set of goals.
Sub-goal 2   Record keeping.
Sub-goal 3   Evaluating your situation on the basis of gathered data.
Sub-goal 4   Setting up graded sub-goals and strategies.
Sub-goal 5   Collecting reinforcers.
Sub-goal 6   Using principles of self-reinforcement.
Sub-goal 7   Progress monitoring and assessment.
Sub-goal 8   Deep relaxation.
Sub-goal 9   Quick relaxation.
Sub-goal 10   Differential relaxation.

Sub-goal one – establishing an overall goal or set of goals

Inability to establish goals correctly is a major obstacle to success. Many people believe that they can state their goals or ambitions adequately when, in fact, they never do so. For example you hear people say: 'I want to get an interesting job . . .' or 'I wish I had more willpower . . .' Ask them if they feel they have expressed a goal and they will probably say they have. Actually they have done nothing of the kind. Describing your goals in this way is rather like saying: 'I want to go on holiday . . .' As a general statement of intent it is fair enough. But only when a specific destination has been decided on can you take the necessary, practical steps needed to realise the goal.

Dissatisfactions are frequently confused with goals. A student finds it hard to study for an exam so he says: 'I wish I was brighter' or 'I wish I had a better memory.' A young housewife feels lonely when she gives up a career outside the home to look after children and complains: 'I wish I had a more satisfying life.' A retired man, frustrated by inactivity after a busy career, grumbles: 'I wish the days didn't drag so.' These are not goals at all – just general complaints about the way life is working out. But even when precisely stated a goal may be too negative or general to implement. The housewife might, for instance, have expressed her dissatisfaction in these terms: 'I wish I wasn't so tied to the home.' The pensioner could have grumbled: 'I wish I didn't feel so bored these days' and been of just as little use.

In the Fourteen-Day Programme which follows we are going to ask you to select a goal from a list of five possible pieces of behaviour modification. They have been chosen not for any particular merit they possess, although each will prove mildly beneficial, but because they are easily monitored. Later on you will be shown how to express complex goals in the correct practical terms. For the moment remember that goal specifying is an important and little used skill, and that most goals are stated in terms which are too general or too negative to be put into effect.

Sub-goal two – record keeping

In order to assess your current situation accurately and have a firm basis from which to make change, you must have reliable information about your present behaviour. Such information is termed *baseline data*.

We very seldom think of our behaviour in precise and measurable terms. We tend to say things like: 'I smoke too much' or 'I don't get on with my husband' or 'I can't do exams'. Record keeping enables us to express such comments in a detailed way which may be used for later behavioural change. For instance we may discover that we smoke thirty-three cigarettes each day and smoke particularly heavily at certain times; that the number of arguments with a husband increases significantly over the weekends; or that sitting down to an examination produces an anxiety rating of one hundred per cent while waiting outside the examination room door provides eighty per cent anxiety on a scale in which zero represents total relaxation.

When keeping records you will be noting such details as the surroundings, including the time, the place and the behaviour of others, your own response and its consequences. In this way you will rapidly be able to build up an overall and accurate picture of how, when and in what circumstances you behave in a certain way.

Records must be kept from the first day of any programme. You can use scraps of paper, a notebook, record cards or a pocket tape recorder. Such on the spot notes should be transferred to the permanent record sheet each evening. Never rely on memory. Note behaviour as and when it happens, if necessary devising your own shorthand to keep the details conveniently brief.

Sub-goal three – evaluating your situation on the basis of gathered data

During the first part of the programme you are going to be asked to observe your behaviour and gather data while making no attempt to change it. This is important in any programme of behaviour modification whether simple or complex. The more complete and accurate this data the more easily will you be able to evaluate your current situation and identify areas where change is needed.

Sub-goal four – setting up graded sub-goals and strategies

When you have specified a goal it is seldom either possible or desirable to make a single jump from the present situation to the desired situation. To attempt to do so can result in failure and loss of confidence in the programme. During the course of the Fourteen-Day Programme you will be shown how to produce a pathway of graded sub-goals and strategies towards the major goal.

Sub-goal five – collecting reinforcers

Reinforcers, as we explained in Part One, are rewards used to establish new pieces of behaviour. During the programme you will be asked first of all to note down things you do which are rewarding. These may be large and fairly expensive rewards, like gifts to yourself, dining out or going to the theatre. Or they can be quite simple; a walk in the fresh air, listening to a piece of music, watching a TV programme, reading a chapter of a new book, buying a magazine and so on.

Sub-goal six – using principles of self-reinforcement

During the programme you will be asked to make use of the reinforcers collected in order to establish new behaviour as we described in Part One.

Sub-goal seven – progress monitoring and assessment

Using the record chart you will be shown how to keep an eye on your progress, assess the rate of behavioural change and make changes in the programme if necessary.

Sub-goal eight – deep relaxation

As we shall see, relaxation is the natural enemy of anxiety and tension because it puts the body into a state of nervous arousal which is directly opposed to that produced by stress. If the body is sufficiently relaxed it is virtually impossible for anxiety symptoms, such as beating heart, a dry mouth and churning stomach, to occur. Relaxation is a vital skill in behaviour control but, in our modern, high speed world where it is most needed, a sadly neglected one. During the course of the programme you will be shown how to relax very deeply.

Sub-goal nine – quick relaxation

This skill is developed directly from the preceding one and is designed for use in situations where anxiety or the effects of stress occur unexpectedly or suddenly. For example just before an important meeting, when confronted by an angry superior, at the start of an important game of golf or tennis.

Sub-goal ten – differential relaxation

This is the ability to relax those parts of the body not being used whilst maintaining tension in working muscles. For example using this skill you will be able to talk to a large group of people without stress because your body, apart from the muscles directly in use, are relaxed and at ease. This skill is especially valuable when playing a sport.

These, then, are the ten skills or sub-goals which will be taught during the Fourteen-Day Programme. If you feel alert and ready to start, and providing you have about forty-five minutes free time available you can begin right away. But remember only read the exercises for the day, on the day you intend to carry them out and stick to our two-week timetable.

Day one

Total time needed – forty-five minutes approximately.

Sub-goals to be practised
Sub-goal one – establishing an overall goal or set of goals
Time required – approximately one minute.
Best time of day – any time.

Sub-goal eight – deep relaxation
Time required – approximately forty-five minutes.
Best time of day – mid-evening or just before going to sleep.

Sub-goal one – establishing an overall goal or set of goals

For practice purposes we want you to pick one of the following goals.
1 Trebling the amount of time which you spend walking each day.
2 Reducing cigarette consumption to one tenth its normal level.
3 Removing bread completely from your diet.
4 Increasing the periods of time spent in conversation with your partner or spouse.
5 Increasing the period of time spent on deep relaxation each day to twice its present level.

These goals have been selected for the ease with which the changes of behaviour involved can be measured. Select the goal which seems most meaningful to you and then try to stick to it during the coming two weeks. We are not suggesting that you genuinely feel the need for change in any of these areas, but simply asking you to adopt one for practice purposes. Even if you are a heavy smoker and want to continue at your present level it might be interesting to pick the second goal simply to prove to yourself that a reduction is possible using behavioural modification methods.

So far as this sub-goal is concerned that is all we want you to do on Day One. Simply make your choice.

Sub-goal eight – deep relaxation

The setting. This should be a quiet room with the curtains drawn and the lights dimmed. It should have a bed, couch or armchair which provides adequate support for the back and neck and sufficient room to stretch out your legs straight. The room temperature should be comfortable and you should loosen any tight clothing.

The procedure. The first step is to read through the whole exercise and familiarise yourself with the methods and the muscle groups which you are going to relax. At first this may seem a little complicated but, by the end of the first session you should have mastered the procedure quite easily. To help you we have divided the groups into six main body areas. These are:

1 Arms and hands.
2 Neck and shoulders.
3 Eyes, eyebrows and forehead.
4 Mouth and throat.
5 Trunk and chest.
6 Legs and hips.

You can remember these by memorising the mnemonic:

All New Exercises Must Take Longer

As you can see the first letter of each word in this phrase stands for one of the six body areas. The mnemonic together with the muscle group cartoons (see diagram 7 on p 59) and a careful reading of the text should enable you to complete the first practice session without difficulty.

The procedure is extremely simple. You concentrate on each of the major muscle groups in the six body areas in turn. By alternately tensing and relaxing them you quickly teach yourself the difference between tension and relaxation. But you must really concentrate on letting the muscles unwind. Even when you think they are relaxed try and let yourself go a little more. Feel the muscles getting heavier and heavier. You should concentrate on each of the muscle groups for about one minute. During this time the muscles may start to tingle and feel slightly cold. Do not worry because this is a perfectly natural and normal part of the relaxation process.

When carrying out the breathing exercises to tense and relax the chest muscles you will see that breathing in produces tension and breathing out relaxation. When relaxing other muscle groups you will be breathing lightly and evenly, but each time you exhale let yourself relax a little more deeply. Learn to associate breathing out with relaxation.

When all the muscle groups have been relaxed, lie still and quiet and try to form a mental image of some tranquil and soothing scene. Perhaps this will be a quiet country landscape, or a warm and deserted beach, a picture of waves slowly uncurling in a tropical bay. Or it could simply be a wash of soft colour. At first you may find it hard to hold this mental scene for more than a few seconds, but with practice it will become easier and easier to use this imagery to increase your sense of well-being and relaxation.

The exercises. Read through these exercises and keep the mnemonic phrase in your mind to help you remember the muscle groups.

All New Exercises Must Take Longer

A Group (arms and hands)

Fists: Clench both fists as tightly as you can for five seconds and feel the tension. Now relax them completely and note the difference between tension and relaxation. Concentrate on letting the muscles unwind for about a minute.

Front upper arms: Now bend your arms at the elbows to tighten the muscles at the front of the upper arm. Hold this position for about five seconds and then relax and let your arms straighten by your sides. Again continue to let the muscles unwind and concentrate on the feeling of letting go for about a minute.

Back upper arms: This time you should straighten your arms as rigidly as you can. Feel the tension in the back of your upper arms for about five seconds and then let go. Flop the arms out and continue to let those muscles unwind for about a minute.

Now take an extra minute and concentrate on all the muscles in the hands and arms, letting them feel more and more deeply relaxed.

N Group (neck and shoulders)

Neck: You can tense these muscles by pressing your head back into the armchair or couch as hard as you can for about five seconds. Feel the tension and then relax your neck and let your head rest back gently. Concentrate on the feeling of letting go for the next minute.

Shoulders: Shrug your shoulders, drawing them up into the neck as tightly as you can and feel the tension in your shoulders. Hold that position for five seconds and then relax. Let your shoulders flop and unwind. Carry on that feeling of letting go for about a minute.

Then continue to let the muscles of your neck, shoulders and arms relax completely for about a minute.

E Group (eyes, eyebrows, forehead)

Eyebrows and eyes: Tense these by frowning as hard as you can and squeezing your eyes tightly shut. Hold that tension for five seconds and then relax. Feel the relief on letting go and continue to smooth out your brow. For the next minute concentrate on these muscles only.

Forehead and scalp: Tense these muscles by raising your eyebrows as though enquiring. Try to raise your eyebrows as high as you can and hold them there for about five seconds. Feel the tension and then relax. Notice the difference between tension and relaxation and continue the feeling of letting go. Keep your eyes still and looking straight ahead.

Now for another minute let the muscles around your eyes, forehead, neck, shoulders and arms relax completely.

M Group (mouth and throat)

Mouth: The muscles in your lips and face can be tensed by pressing the lips lightly together. Hold this position for five seconds and then relax. Let your lips rest lightly together and continue the feeling of letting go for about one minute.

Jaw: Can be tensed by biting the teeth together for about five seconds. Feel the tension in your jaw and then relax the muscles. Part your teeth slightly so there is no tension in your jaw and feel the relief of letting go for the next minute.

Throat: These muscles can be tensed by putting the tip of your tongue against the roof of your mouth and pressing upwards as hard as you can for about five seconds. Feel the tension in your tongue and throat and then let go. Feel the relief of letting go and let your tongue flop down into the bottom of your mouth. Continue the feeling of relaxation for about a minute.

T Group (trunk and chest)

Chest: Take in a deep breath and hold that breath for about five seconds. Feel the tension in the chest and then breathe out and concentrate on the feeling of letting go. Then take another deep breath. Feel the tension. Hold it for five seconds and then relax. Breathe out and let go. Now keep your breathing shallow and relaxed as before. But every time you breathe out feel the relief of letting go. Continue to practise this for the next minute.

Stomach: Tighten the muscles around your stomach area as though you were preparing to receive a blow. Feel the tension as they are tight and rigid. Hold that position for about five seconds. Now relax and let your stomach muscles flop and relax. Continue the feeling of letting go for the next minute.

Now for a further minute concentrate on letting go all the muscles of the trunk, neck, face and arms.

L Group (legs and hips)

Legs: Tense these by squeezing your thighs and buttocks together, straightening your legs and pointing your toes downwards. Hold that position for five seconds. Feel the tension in your legs and hips and then relax completely. Feel the tension ease away from your legs and hips and continue to let go and unwind for the next minute.

Whole body: For the next two or three minutes concentrate on relaxing all the major muscles. Feel yourself sinking deeper and deeper into the bed, couch or chair as your body becomes heavier and heavier, more and more deeply relaxed. During this period close your eyes and try to conjure up the pleasant image. Hold it in your mind as vividly as possible and feel it making you more and more relaxed. After a few minutes open your eyes and *slowly* move your body around. Now sit up and return to your normal routine.

This ends the work for Day One. Read the first exercise for Day Two as early as possible tomorrow morning. Now please close the book.

Day two

Total time needed – thirty minutes approximately.

Sub-goal to be consolidated
Sub-goal eight – deep relaxation
Time required – as before but try to reduce to approximately thirty minutes.

New sub-goal to be practised
Sub-goal two – record keeping
Time required – varies with goal chosen.
Best time of day – when behaviour occurs.

Sub-goal eight – deep relaxation

Go through the same exercises as in Day One but try to rely more on memory (use the mnemonic phrase) than by referring to the book. Work slowly through all the muscle groups, tensing and relaxing each group in turn. Try to strengthen the pleasant image which you have at the end of the exercises and see whether you can relax more and more deeply. If possible keep your eyes closed throughout the exercise period.

Sub-goal two – record keeping

Today and on subsequent days you will be recording information about your behaviour in relation to the goal which you selected yesterday. To do this you will need a small notebook or pad with the pages set out as in Diagram 3 page 40. Under each of the headings you will be noting the following baseline data:

1 Stimulus
This refers to the surroundings in which you find yourself when carrying out the target behaviour. You must note where you are, the time of day, your own activities up to that point and the activities of others. You can use any simple abbreviations to keep the record short, but make certain it is accurate. If you have understood the behavioural terms defined in Section One you will see that what you are recording are the *stimulus control* situations under which you smoke, walk, eat bread, relax or speak to your partner.

2 Response
This refers to the number of times you have carried out a piece of behaviour or the amount of time taken over it, as well as what the response was. For example if your target is to reduce the number of cigarettes smoked then you will note the number of cigarettes smoked under the stimulus situation. If the goal is an increase in time spent talking to a partner or spouse then you will note the approximate length of time spent in conversation. The examples given in Diagrams 1/2/3/4/5/6 will make this point clear.

3 Consequence

What happened immediately after you carried out the piece of target behaviour must be noted. What was the effect on yourself and your surroundings? How did others respond?

4 Reinforcers

This heading is to be left blank for the moment. It will be used as from Day Three.

It is important that you record the behaviour as you carry it out and not rely on memory to make up the notes at the end of the day. At the end of the day, however, you must total up the number of behaviours which occurred under the *Response* heading. In the case of goal two this will be the total number of cigarettes smoked, in the bread reduction goal the total number of slices eaten and in the other three instances you will note down the total time spent on each activity. *At this stage make no attempt to change your normal behaviours.* Merely act as a detached observer noting accurate information about the way you behave.

This concludes the exercises to be practised on Day Two. Day Three will involve work on three skills. As two of them have to be carried out during the course of the day, read the instructions as early as possible tomorrow. Now please close the book.

Day three

Total time needed – thirty-five minutes approximately.

Sub-goals to be consolidated
Sub-goal two – record keeping
Sub-goal eight – deep relaxation
Carry out as before and try to reduce the time it takes to relax deeply.

New sub-goal to be practised
Sub-goal five – collecting reinforcers
Time required – about five minutes.
Best time of day – when the situation arises.

Sub-goal two and sub-goal eight

These sub-goals are to be carried out as before. Keep your record charts up to date and, at the end of the day, note the number of incidents of the behaviour being monitored or the amount of time taken up by this behaviour. At this stage you should be able to relax without reference to the instructions and it should be easier to hold a strong mental image at the end of the twenty minute period.

Sub-goal five – collecting reinforcers

For this sub-goal you will be making use of the fourth column on your record sheet. Note down at any moment during the day, the things you do which give you pleasure. You should include items which occur fairly frequently and are short lasting as well as infrequent and lengthy pleasures, for example going to the theatre or cinema or visiting a friend, although these may be more difficult to use in this current programme. Especially useful types of short-term positive reinforcers include making a telephone call to a friend or relative, having coffee and biscuits, buying a favourite magazine, reading a chapter in a new book, putting your feet up and watching a TV programme, having a drink. There will be very many more in your own behaviour. You should include them no matter how small or trivial they seem. They are *your* personal reinforcers and it is only as far as you are concerned that they need be considered as rewarding.

This concludes the exercises to be practised on Day Three. Try and read the instructions for Day Four as early as possible tomorrow morning. Now please close the book.

Day four

Consolidation of skills

Today we want you to concentrate on practising the sub-goals already explained. Relaxation should be getting increasingly easy and rewarding by now and your record charts should be detailed

Diagram one – Example of record keeping chart for fourteen-day behaviour modification programme

Goal –

Day –

Stimulus	Response	Consequence	Reinforcer
Surroundings in which behaviour was carried out. Where you are. Time of day. Activities carried on by you and others. Use of shorthand if necessary to keep short, but do not sacrifice accuracy for brevity	What you did. How long it took or number of items involved.	What happened immediately after behaviour was carried out. What you did. How you felt. How did the people around you respond?	Leave blank on Day Two.

Total number of times activity being monitored was carried out (i.e. number of cigarettes smoked, slices of bread eaten, or the total amount of time spent walking, talking or relaxing.)

Diagram two – Typical entries in record chart if goal (1) chosen

Goal – Trebling the amount of time which you spend walking each day

Day – ONE

Stimulus	Response	Consequence	Reinforcer
8.30 a.m. At home about to start for the office. Fine morning. Think about walking to the station.	Walk to the station. 10 mins.	Felt slightly hot and out of breath when got there.	
11.15 a.m. Needed to see client across the city. Could walk but seems too hot.	Took cab.	Arrived late for appointment due to traffic.	
1.15 p.m. Lunch.	Walked to nearby restaurant. 4 mins.	Arrived feeling relaxed and hungry.	
5.30 p.m. Leaving work.	Took bus to the station.	Hot and crowded.	
6.45 p.m. Leaving station. Wife not there to meet me.	Felt irritated and walked home. 10 mins.	Arrived feeling in good humour. Felt the exercise had done me good.	

Total time spent walking – approximately 24 minutes on DAY ONE

Diagram three – Typical entries in record chart if goal (2) is chosen

Goal – Reducing cigarette consumption to one tenth its normal level

Day – ONE

Stimulus	Response	Consequence	Reinforcer
8.15 a.m. At home. Just finished breakfast. Feeling miserable. Raining.	Smoked first cigarette.	Felt less depressed.	
9.00 a.m. On tube to work. Crowded. Thought of day ahead. Daunting.	Smoked two cigarettes on journey.	Enjoyed them and felt more relaxed.	
10.00 a.m. With colleague working out schedule in office. He offered me cigarettes.	Smoked three. Two his, one mine.	Enjoyed sharing cigarettes. Worked more efficiently.	
11.30 a.m. Waiting to see Managing Director. Tense.	Smoked one cigarette.	Felt less anxious.	
12.00. Felt tired after meeting. Went for some air in the street, etc, etc.	Smoked two cigarettes.	Gradually unwound.	

Total cigarettes smoked – 30 on DAY ONE

Diagram four – Typical entries in record chart if goal (3) is chosen

Goal – Removing bread completely from your diet

Day – ONE

Stimulus	Response	Consequence	Reinforcer
8.00 a.m. Breakfast alone. In rush to eat.	Had tea and three slices of white bread (toast) to fill me up.	Hunger gone.	
1.15 p.m. Lunch. In canteen.	Four slices of bread with fish and chips and tea.	Felt pleasantly full.	
6.00 p.m. At home. Preparing evening meal.	Had two slices of toast with fish paste and coffee.	Felt less tired.	
8.30 p.m. Supper. Stew shared with friend	Ate one slice of bread.	Enjoyed meal.	

Total slices eaten – 10 on DAY ONE

Diagram five – Typical entries in record chart if goal (4) is chosen

Goal – Increasing the period of time spent in conversation with your partner or spouse

Day – ONE

Stimulus	Response	Consequence	Reinforcer
8.15 a.m. Breakfast in the living room. Husband reading the paper.	Talked about a friend who was coming to see me. About 5 mins.	Not very interested. Went on reading the paper. Nodded and muttered from time to time.	
1.30. Lunch. Husband at home.	Chatted about his morning. Asked me when friend was coming over. 10 mins.	Relaxed and pleasant feeling.	
6.30 p.m. Husband home and tired. Came into kitchen.	Talked for about 5 mins.	Felt irritated about being interrupted at work.	
8.30 p.m. Dinner at home. TV on.	Talked for about 10 mins.	Neither of us seemed to want to talk. Good programme on.	
10.30 p.m. Getting ready for bed.	Talked about tomorrow and visit by friend. 10 mins.	Both felt tired.	

Total amount of time spent talking to husband – approximately 40 minutes on DAY ONE

Diagram six – Typical entries in record chart if goal (5) is chosen

Goal – Increasing the period of time spent on deep relaxation each day to twice its present level

Day – ONE

Stimulus	Response	Consequence	Reinforcer
7.30 p.m. Have read DAY ONE relaxation in 14-Day Programme again. At home in the lounge.	Try to relax for about 20 mins.	Feel better but get bored and spend only 15 mins.	
10.30 p.m. In bed at home.	Decide to attempt relaxation again. Spend full 20 mins doing exercises.	Feel very relaxed and ready for sleep.	

Total amount of time spent relaxing – 35 minutes on DAY ONE

and accurate. Make certain that you are building up a good supply of reinforcers in the fourth column. It may also be valuable to re-read the list of behavioural definitions given at the end of Part One. Perhaps some of these terms have now taken on a new meaning as you experience the reality of the skills to which we referred. It is important that you can relate your practical experience of behaviour monitoring with the theoretical definitions.

Because today you are only repeating previously learned skills and not adding to them do not think that the work is unimportant. Consolidation of skills is so essential to developing new patterns of behaviour that it could be considered a sub-goal in itself.

This concludes the exercises to be practised today. Now please close the book.

Day five

Total time needed – fifty-five minutes approximately.

Sub-goals to be consolidated
Sub-goal two – record keeping
Sub-goal five – collecting reinforcers
Sub-goal eight – deep relaxation

New sub-goals to be practised
Sub-goal three – evaluating your situation on the basis of gathered data
Time required – approximately fifteen minutes.
Best time of day – end of the day.

Sub-goal four – the setting up of graded sub-goals and strategies
Time required – about ten minutes.
Best time of day – end of the day.

Sub-goal two – record keeping

By the end of today you will have collected baseline data about the piece of behaviour you have been monitoring over a four day period. In Sub-Goal Four you will make use of this data to construct a pathway from the current situation to the desired situation. But keep on with the recording even while you are modifying your behaviour. The new data will enable you to evaluate your progress towards the overall goal.

Sub-goal five – collecting reinforcers

You should now have a number of rewarding situations noted in column four of your record chart. You will start using some of these from tomorrow. On the back of the chart make a list of six minor reinforcers which can be frequently and fairly quickly carried out, for example drinking coffee, phoning a friend, or reading a magazine. Also note down two more involved and lengthier reinforcers, such as eating out, going to the theatre, etc.

Sub-goal eight – deep relaxation

During today's session try and increase the speed at which you can relax. Now that you have learned the difference between tension and relaxation you may find it possible to relax without the prior tightening of the muscles. See if you can get some of the muscle groups to relax immediately.

Sub-goal three – evaluating your situation on the basis of gathered data

In order to get an overall picture of your current rate of response in your chosen target area you should now take the previous four days' records and extract an average figure which represents current baseline behaviour. Simply total your daily behaviour scores and divide by four. This figure will represent your present situation and will determine the point from which you start your behaviour modification programme.

Example One: Amount of time spent walking during four days of monitoring

Day two	Day three	Day four	Day five
24 minutes	18 minutes	14 minutes	20 minutes

Total time spent walking = 76 minutes.
Average (*divide by 4*)   = 19 minutes per day.
The goal is to treble the amount of time spent walking, so that by Day Thirteen of the modification programme you will be walking for about fifty-seven minutes per day.

Example two: Number of cigarettes smoked during four days of monitoring

Day two	Day three	Day four	Day five
30	35	28	37

Total number smoked = 130.
Average (*divide by 4*) = 32 cigarettes per day.
The goal is to reduce the daily cigarette consumption to three per day by Day Thirteen of the programme.

Example three: Amount of bread eaten during four days of monitoring

Day two	Day three	Day four	Day five
8 slices	12 slices	10 slices	10 slices

Total number of slices eaten = 40.
Average (*divide by 4*)   = 10 slices per day.
The goal is to eliminate all bread from the diet by Day Thirteen of the programme.

Example four: Amount of time spent talking to spouse during four days of monitoring

Day two	Day three	Day four	Day five
40 minutes	25 minutes	39 minutes	56 minutes

Total time spent talking = 160 minutes.
Average (*divide by 4*)   = 40 minutes per day.
A realistic goal would be to double the amount of time up to eighty minutes per day.

Example five: Amount of time spent on deep relaxation during four days of monitoring

Day two	Day three	Day four	Day five
45 minutes	38 minutes	47 minutes	50 minutes

Total time spent relaxing = 180 minutes.
Average (*divide by 4*)   = 45 minutes per day.
The goal is to double the amount of time spent relaxing each day to ninety minutes.

Sub-goal four – the setting up of graded sub-goals and strategies

Having established desired behaviour and current behaviour scores it is now necessary to structure a graded path between the two over the next eight days. The first step is to write down on your record sheet the average number, representing your current behaviour, as calculated in Sub-Goal Three. Leave space below this for seven further entries and then enter the desired target figure. In the case of bread eating this will be 0. In all other cases this final figure will depend on your current baseline score. Now work out a carefully graded pathway to this goal. The intermediate increases or decreases of behaviour can be likened to stepping stones across a river. If you put them too close together progress may be too slow to achieve the desired target within the time allowed. If you are too ambitious and place them too far apart you risk failure and a loss of confidence in your ability to effect a change. You may find it useful to take smaller steps initially and gradually increase them towards the end of the programme. The examples given below will serve as a guide when fixing daily targets for the next eight days of the programme.

Example one
Average amount of time spent walking during four days of monitoring = 19 minutes
Goal: To increase this amount of time to 57 minutes per day over eight days
Graded pathway:

Day five . . . . 19 minutes per day (current situation)
Day six . . . . 22 minutes per day
Day seven . . . . 26 minutes per day
Day eight . . . . 31 minutes per day
Day nine . . . . 36 minutes per day   Increase in
Day ten . . . . 41 minutes per day   behaviour
Day eleven . . . . . . 46 minutes per day
Day twelve . . . . . . 51 minutes per day
Day thirteen . . . . . 57 minutes per day (goal or desired situation)

Example two
Average number of cigarettes smoked during four days of
monitoring = 32
Goal: To reduce daily cigarette consumption to three over
eight days
Graded pathway:
Day five . . . . 32 cigarettes smoked (current situation)
Day six . . . . 29 cigarettes smoked
Day seven . . . . 26 cigarettes smoked
Day eight . . . . 22 cigarettes smoked
Day nine . . . . 18 cigarettes smoked   Decrease in
Day ten . . . . 14 cigarettes smoked   behaviour
Day eleven . . . . . . 10 cigarettes smoked
Day twelve . . . . . . 6 cigarettes smoked
Day thirteen . . . . . 3 cigarettes smoked (goal or desired situation)

Example three
Average amount of bread eaten during four days of
monitoring = 10 slices
Goal: To eliminate bread from the diet over eight days
Graded pathway:
Day five . . . . 10 slices eaten (current situation)
Day six . . . . 9 slices eaten
Day seven . . . . 8 slices eaten
Day eight . . . . 6 slices eaten
Day nine . . . . 4 slices eaten   Decrease in
Day ten . . . . 3 slices eaten   behaviour
Day eleven . . . . . . 2 slices eaten
Day twelve . . . . . . 1 slice eaten
Day thirteen . . . . . 0 – bread removed from diet (goal or desired
                           situation)

Example four
Average amount of time spent talking to spouse during four days
of monitoring = 40 minutes
Goal: To increase this period of time to 80 minutes daily
over eight days
Graded pathway:

Day five ....40 minutes per day (current situation)
Day six ....44 minutes per day
Day seven ....48 minutes per day
Day eight ....53 minutes per day
Day nine ....58 minutes per day   Increase in
Day ten ....63 minutes per day   behaviour
Day eleven ......68 minutes per day
Day twelve ......74 minutes per day
Day thirteen .....80 minutes per day (goal or desired situation)

Example five
Average amount of time spent on deep relaxation during
four days of monitoring = 45 minutes
Goal: To increase the amount of time spent relaxing to
90 minutes per day
Graded pathway:

Day five ....45 minutes per day (current situation)
Day six ....48 minutes per day
Day seven ....52 minutes per day
Day eight ....57 minutes per day
Day nine ....62 minutes per day   Increase in
Day ten ....68 minutes per day   behaviour
Day eleven   75 minutes per day
Day twelve ......82 minutes per day
Day thirteen .....90 minutes per day (goal or desired situation)

Note that you must space out the stages by which you increase or decrease a piece of behaviour as evenly as possible, being perhaps more cautious at the start because, as you gain confidence in your ability to adjust your behaviour, it will become easier to take slightly bolder steps. But never attempt too much too quickly or you may fail and, in failing, lose confidence in the programme.

This concludes the work for Day Five of the programme. Tomorrow you will start to modify your behaviour by taking the first step towards the desired situation. To help you do this you will use the self-reinforcers which you have been collecting. For this reason it will be useful to read the first part of your instructions for Day Six as early on as possible, preferably before you get out of bed. Now close the book.

Day six

Sub-goal to be consolidated
Sub-goal two – record keeping
Continue as before.

New sub-goals to be practised
Sub-goal six – using principles of self-reinforcement
Time required – approximately ten minutes.
Best time of day – throughout the day.

Sub-goal nine – quick relaxation
Time required – two sessions of ten minutes duration.
Best time of day – middle of day and last thing at night.

Sub-goal six – using principles of self-reinforcement

Procedure: The object of this sub-goal is to help you reach your target behaviour for the day, whether this is cutting down the number of cigarettes smoked from, say, thirty-two to twenty-nine, reducing the amount of bread eaten from, say, ten to eight; slices or increasing the amount of time spent talking to your spouse from forty minutes to forty-five minutes.

Depending on the goal you selected on Day Two, you are going to have to increase a piece of behaviour (walking, talking and relaxing) or decrease a piece of behaviour (smoking, bread eating). In both cases the method is the same. From your list of reinforcers select some which can be practically applied *immediately* after achieving the desired target. Naturally you must not reward yourself for not smoking by having a cigarette!

Example one
Overall goal: to increase time spent walking from nineteen to fifty-seven minutes per day.
Target for Day Six of programme: increase from nineteen to twenty-two minutes. Target achieved by walking back from client instead of taking cab.
Reinforcer chosen: spend cab fare on buying wanted paperback.
Reinforcer applied: immediately on returning to office area.

Example two
Overall goal: to reduce cigarettes smoked from an average of thirty-two to three per day.
Target for Day Six of programme: decrease from thirty-two to twenty-nine. Target achieved by cutting out smoking on journey to work (2), and by not smoking between lunch and mid-afternoon break (1).
Reinforcers chosen: purchase of magazine and fifteen minutes instead of ten minutes break mid-afternoon.
Reinforcers applied: on arrival at destination in the morning. Mid-afternoon.

Example three
Overall goal: to decrease total amount of bread eaten each day from an average of ten slices per day to zero.
Target for Day Six of programme: from ten to nine. Target achieved by cutting out bread with afternoon tea.
Reinforcers chosen: phoned friend and chatted for ten minutes.
Reinforcers applied: immediately after afternoon tea.

Example four
Overall goal: to increase the amount of time spent talking to spouse from an average of forty minutes per day to eighty minutes per day.

Target for Day Six of programme: from forty minutes to forty-four minutes. Target achieved by going in to lounge to talk with husband and make him a drink when he got back from work.
Reinforcer chosen: ten minutes pottering around the garden.
Reinforcer applied: immediately after conversation.

Example five
Overall goal: to increase amount of time spent on deep relaxation from an average of forty-five minutes per day to ninety minutes per day.
Target for Day Six of programme: from forty-five to forty-eight minutes. Target achieved during evening period of relaxation.
Reinforcer chosen: listening to favourite piece of music.
Reinforcer applied: immediately after each relaxation session.

In your records you will, of course, note these changes in behaviour under the *Response* heading. You will also note your chosen reinforcer under the fourth heading.

Remember that for a reinforcer to be effective it must follow the piece of target behaviour immediately. Any delay between carrying out the desired behaviour and rewarding yourself for doing so will weaken the power of the reinforcer.

Sub-goal nine – quick relaxation

Procedure: Sit down in a quiet room, tense all your muscles; clench your fists, bend your arms at the elbows as though trying to touch your wrists to your shoulders, shrug your shoulders, press your head back against the chair and tense your neck, squeeze your eyes tightly shut, clench your teeth and press your lips together; straighten your legs and lift your heels slightly off the floor to tense your stomach muscles. Take in a deep breath. Hold all this for five seconds and then literally flop out, letting everything relax as quickly and deeply as you can. Stay like this, concentrating on your relaxing image for ten minutes. Carry out this task twice during the day.

This concludes the exercises for Day Six. Now please close the book.

Day seven

Consolidation of skills

Today will be spent carrying out the previously learned sub-goals of record keeping, using principles of self-reinforcement and quick relaxation.

You will slightly increase, or decrease your selected behaviour over Day Six to reach the graded sub-goal of behaviour. Ensure that, by the end of today, you have achieved the set target.

Make certain that every time you reach the target you reward yourself immediately.

At this time you may find that your gradually more controlled behaviour is providing you with a small amount of stress. This is normal in the early stages of behavioural control and you should consider it to be a positive sign rather than a negative one. However, the effects of such stress can be considerably reduced by the use, whenever the tension arises, of quick relaxation.

This concludes the work for Day Seven. Now please close the book.

Day eight

Sub-goals to be consolidated
Sub-goal two – record keeping
Sub-goal six – using principles of self-reinforcement
Sub-goal nine – quick relaxation

New sub-goal to be practised
Sub-goal seven – progress monitoring and assessment
Time required – approximately five minutes.
Best time of day – towards the end of the day.

Sub-goal seven – progress monitoring and assessment

At this stage of the programme you must make an assessment of your progress towards the overall goal by comparing the target behaviour for each day against what has actually been achieved.

Is your behaviour either increasing or decreasing in line with the stages set on Day Five of the programme? If you have fallen behind make an all-out effort tomorrow to bring your behaviour back into line with the target. It is unwise to allow discrepancies between the two to mount up because the less actual attainment tallies with predicted behaviour the less confidence you will retain in the programme.

Continue to increase the speed and ease with which you can relax. Practise quick relaxation at odd moments during the day so that you can switch to a relaxed state within a matter of seconds.

This concludes the tasks for Day Eight. Now please close the book.

Day nine

Consolidation of skills

Today continue record keeping, using principles of self-reinforcement, to establish new behaviour and quick relaxation. We also want you to spend one twenty-minute period practising deep relaxation. Make certain that records are being kept accurately.

If there is any discrepancy between predicted target and attained target make an all-out effort today to bring your behaviour into line.

This concludes the work for Day Nine of the programme. Now please close the book.

Day ten

Consolidation of skills

Today you will continue to keep records, assess your progress and use self-reinforcers to establish the desired pieces of behaviour which are helping you towards the overall goal.

Quick relaxation should be practised whenever possible. Use any few moments of free time to do this. It will bring a general feeling of well-being.

At the end of the day check your totals against today's target. If there is a discrepancy make a special effort tomorrow to close the gap. Now that you are skilled at relaxation, and more experienced in the use of self-reinforcers you should find this fairly easy. If quick relaxation is enjoyable there is no reason why you should not use this as a reinforcer for all goals with the exception of increasing deep relaxation.

This concludes the instructions for Day Ten. Now please close the book.

Day eleven

Sub-goals to be consolidated
Sub-goal seven – progress monitoring and assessment
Sub-goal nine – quick relaxation
Two periods at least to be carried out.

New sub-goal to be practised
Sub-goal ten – differential relaxation
Time required – about five minutes.
Best time of day – after quick relaxation.

Sub-goal ten – differential relaxation

The main difference between differential relaxation and the other types of relaxation is that you can carry out this technique while moving around. It is especially useful, as we noted earlier, when playing a sport, speaking in public or attending interviews. Any piece of behaviour, in fact, where you need to stay cool and collected while involved in physical or mental effort.

After one of the two quick relaxation sessions open your eyes, but keep the rest of your body relaxed and motionless. Now look around the room. Take in every detail of your surroundings, but move only your eyes. Now start slowly talking to yourself. Say anything you like, but get used to the feeling of speaking while remaining completely relaxed. After a few moments begin to move your arms. Feel the new sensation of moving some of your muscles while the rest of the body remains relaxed. Be sure you are keeping your legs and torso relaxed. Now stand up slowly. Start to walk around the room. Keep those muscles which are not being used in a relaxed state. After a couple of minutes go back to the chair or couch and relax all your muscles again for a few more minutes. This will conclude your first session of differential relaxation.

The work for Day Eleven is also concluded here. Now please close the book.

Day twelve

Consolidation of skills

Keep using self-reinforcements to reward yourself for achieving target behaviour. Make sure you are still taking an accurate record of your behaviour as it is modified in line with the overall goal. Practise the relaxation skills regularly and try to use quick relaxation several times a day, at home, at work, and, perhaps, while travelling to work. Use it too just before any potentially stressful occasion, for example an important meeting with clients, before an interview or playing a sport. Remember that by tomorrow you should have attained your target goal and either reduced or increased your behaviour to the predicted amount.

This concludes the work for Day Twelve. We suggest you read the instructions for Day Thirteen fairly early in the morning. Now please close the book.

Day thirteen

By the end of the day you should have achieved your target. Your behaviour, if you have carried out the programme correctly, will have been mildly and beneficially modified. During the course of the day carry on with the record taking, self-reinforcement and relaxation. At the end of the day carry out Sub-Goal Seven and evaluate how you have done. If you have achieved the predicted overall goal and cut down your smoking or bread eating, increased your walking, relaxation or conversation by the required amount then reward yourself by using one of the two major reinforcers which you noted on your list of reinforcers.

If you are still just off target then make an all-out attempt to bring your attainments into line during the final day of the programme.

This concludes the work for Day Thirteen. We suggest that you read the instructions for the final day of the programme fairly early tomorrow. Now please close the book.

Day fourteen

Final day of the programme

During today practise relaxation to keep yourself skilled in this valuable procedure. If you are still short of your overall goal try and bring your behaviour into line today, the last day of the programme. If by the end of the day you have succeeded in attaining the goal set nine days ago then we suggest you give yourself some special reward. If you have saved money on smoking, bread eating or transport why not spend it on a present for yourself?

Whether or not you have been able to achieve the overall goal, this fourteen-day programme will have been valuable in teaching you the basic skills of behaviour modification.

The goals we selected, whilst mildly beneficial, were chosen because they were easy to monitor and constructing a graded pathway of sub-goals was relatively simple. The goals which you select for yourself in Part Four of this book are likely to be much more complex and significant. The point to remember is that the procedures will remain the same no matter what goal you select. The first step is to work out a goal which, when attained, will bring fulfilment. Next you will gather *baseline data* so that you have a starting point of accurate information about the way you behave, the frequency with which you show that response and under what circumstances you act in a particular way. Once this baseline data has been gathered the overall goal is then sub-divided into a number of sub-goals; how many depends on the complexity of the ultimate goal. These are the stepping stones towards success.

At the start of this part of the book we looked very briefly at the problem of goal setting and said then that it is an inability to state their goals in life correctly which prevents many people from realising their true potential.

In the next part of this book we will deal at length with the procedures for teasing realistic goals out of a general tangle of dissatisfactions and show you how to state them in such a way that they can be attained.

Diagram seven – Muscle tension and relaxation

Fists clenched tenses the hands

Fist relaxed

Biceps tensed arms bent at elbow

Biceps relaxed

Triceps tensed straightens the arm

Triceps relaxed let arms flop

Grit the teeth tenses the jaw

Part the teeth relaxes the jaw

Press the lips together tenses lips and the facial muscles

Rest lips lightly together relaxes lips and facial muscles

Press tip of tongue against roof of mouth tenses tongue & throat

Let tongue flop relaxes tongue and throat

Press head back, tenses neck

Let head rest back relaxes neck

Shrug shoulders

Relax shoulders

Straighten legs and point toes down tenses legs and toes

Let legs flop and feel legs and toes relax

Breathe in deeply tenses the chest

Breathe out feel the chest relax

Pull stomach muscles in. Tenses stomach

Let stomach muscles out. Relaxes stomach

Tense the buttocks together

Let the buttocks relax

Part three

Eight-day self-analysis programme

Day One consists of a basic analysis of your ambitions and an explanation of the techniques for correctly specifying goals. In a special analysis section you will be shown how to locate any obstacles to fulfilment. The reasons why such obstacles arise and the methods for overcoming them will be explained.

During Days Two to Eight you will be carrying out detailed record keeping in order to gather baseline data about behaviour relevant to the attainment of your goal.

The overall goal of Part Three is to help you expand your awareness of your present lifestyle, to locate obstacles to fulfilment and to discover how and when these arise.

As with the Fourteen-Day Programme you are asked to read this part of the book as instructed.

Day one

The overall goal for Day One is:

To help you expand your awareness of your present lifestyle and locate areas of difficulty.

To achieve this you will need to carry out the following sub-goals:

1 Identifying possible goals.
2 Specifying goals correctly.
3 Identifying barriers to success.
4 Understanding how these barriers arise and how they can be removed.
5 Understanding how to carry out a detailed self-analysis.

Time required – approximately ninety minutes.

Sub-goal one – identifying possible goals

The starting point is an analysis of your present attitudes and aspirations based on the following goal statement inventory. Read down the list of one hundred statements and note the letter in brackets of any with which you feel agreement.

I would like to be able to:

Earn more money in my spare time (A).

Co-operate better with my marriage partner at home (B).

Help in local politics (D).

Ask others for help when I need it at work (C).

Play my favourite sport more effectively (D).

Have my children behave with greater consideration for my feelings and wishes (B).

Refuse extra work in the office when such a refusal is justified (A).

Find interesting things to do in my spare time (D).

Be able to flirt more easily (C).

Remember facts and figures more easily during meetings (A).

Be more open and expressive in my relationship with the opposite sex (B).

Feel more confident in developing new interests in my free time (D).

Welcome extra responsibility in my work (A).

Say 'no' to requests which are unreasonable at home (B).
Sustain my interest in my hobby (D).
Feel more enthusiasm for my work (A).
Gain more satisfaction from sex (B).
Plan my day so that I have more time for leisure (D).
Deal with interviews, holding them or attending them, more effectively (A).
Give compliments and show affection for my partner (B).
Get rid of anxieties about masturbation (B).
Accept praise and compliments graciously (C).
Relate more easily to my colleagues away from work (A).
Be at ease in a party situation (C).
Extend the range of my sexual enjoyments (B).
Give formal lectures or talks (A).
Cope with spectators when playing a sport (D).
Be more convincing in my approach to clients or customers (A).
Have a sexual outlet for my particular needs (B).
Rate my potential more highly as a socialiser (C)
Take a course of further education in my spare time (D).
Feel more confident of my position in my job (A).
Be more confident in my relationships with members of the opposite sex (B).
Perform better under test conditions (A).
Feel more quickly at ease in social situations (C).
Show my emotions more freely with my partner (B).
Delegate responsibility and make my staff more enthusiastic (A).
Pick up my game quickly when I am playing badly (D).
Rate my ambitions more highly in the working situation (A).
Make people feel supported in my company (C).
Become more confident with animals (D).
Break into conversations when entering a room full of people (C).
Gain faster promotion at work (A).
Be able to assert my rights at work (A).
Hold my family parties more easily (B).
Deal with very high work loads without stress (A).
Feel confident that I can engage in interesting conversation (C).
Plan for the increase in leisure time in my retirement (D).
Relate more easily to my relatives (B).

Jolly things along when a sour note has appeared (C).
Look forward to sexual relationships more than I do (B).
Give praise and compliments when appropriate (C).
Be more positive when answering the telephone (A).
Deal with boring conversationalists effectively (C).
Have more harmonious intimate relationships (B).
Develop a meaningful hobby or pastime (D).
Deal with criticism in my work effectively (A).
Develop a winning instinct in sport (D).
Feel more self-confident in social situations (C).
Travel or take holidays without anxiety (D).
Present my work more effectively at meetings with colleagues and
superiors (A).
Build up an absorbing interest during the next few months (D).
Perform better with my sexual partner (B).
Attract and hold the attention of others (C).
Feel more relaxed in competitive sports (D).
Be less inhibited about discussing sex (B).
Keep control of my staff and gain their respect (A).
Become involved in community work (D).
Deal with personal criticism in social situations (C).
Develop a creative talent such as painting or writing (D).
Develop shared interests with my marriage partner (B).
Gain the respect and friendship of people I know socially (C).
Chat more easily in informal situations (C).
Be in better physical shape (D).
Concentrate on work projects more efficiently (A).
Tell a joke effectively in social groups (C).
Find a more stimulating job with greater scope for initiative (A).
Deal more effectively with injustices against me (C).
Concentrate more effectively on sports and pastimes (D).
Have a better relationship with my spouse and children (B).
Give an informal talk easily (C).
Motivate myself easily in my spare time interests (D).
Organise an efficient work programme for myself and my staff (A).
Be more interesting to the opposite sex (B).
Give enjoyable parties for friends (C).
Demonstrate affection in appropriate situations (B).

Start developing spare time interests (D).
Set myself a realistic timetable of work at my leisure or hobby (D).
Cope with high sexual demands on me (B).
Rate my abilities more highly at my sport or hobby (D).
Be better at beginning new relationships with members of the opposite sex (B).
Surmount early difficulties when starting a new hobby or sport (D).
Rate myself more highly sexually (B).
Deal more effectively with excessive invasions of my privacy (C).
Leave work behind at the office (A).
Stand up for my rights and complain when justified in my close relationships (B).
Start conversations with strangers (C).
Discuss my innermost feelings with an intimate partner (B).
Be able to show my feelings more easily with friends (C).
Be better tempered with my work colleagues (A).

Now total the number of As, Bs, Cs and Ds which you have noted down. This will indicate to you which of four life areas most interests you.

A predominance of As suggests that your chief interest at the moment is to be found in the life area of *work and study*.

A predominance of Bs suggests that your chief interest at the moment is to be found in the life area of *family, marriage, sex and intimacy*.

A predominance of Cs suggests that your chief interest at the moment is to be found in the life area of *social and interpersonal relationships*.

A predominance of Ds suggests that your chief interest at the moment is to be found in the life area of *leisure and sports*.

It may be that you have a high score in more than one life area. If this has happened concentrate first on the life area which has the highest score.

The main purpose of this inventory is to guide your thinking towards the correct way of specifying a goal. If you read back over the list you will find that each of the goal statements has three characteristics:

1 It is specific.
2 It is positive.
3 It locates the goal within some environment or situation.

Sub-goal two – specifying goals correctly

Let us look at these important goal-specifying rules in greater detail. Remember that the whole success of any behaviour change programme depends on your ability to state goals in a positive and precise manner.

1 A goal must be specific

You sometimes hear people express goals in these terms:

'I would like to be more successful in life.'
'I wish I was a better person.'

Both these goals have been incorrectly stated because they are too general. Does the first speaker mean material success or greater intellectual achievement? Would they equate success with living quietly but happily or do they want a constant change and excitement? Does 'better' in the second case imply a more charitable outlook towards others, or greater confidence in expressing their own viewpoint?

Be precise. The goal-statement inventory will have helped to direct your mind to one or possibly two life areas in which you have a personal interest. Perhaps some of the statements came very close to expressing your own ambitions. If not, try and use them as a guide to specifying two or three goals in a clear-cut way. One guide as to whether or not you have specified a goal correctly is to ask yourself – 'Can I measure the performance which would lead me towards my achieving the goal?'

During the Fourteen-Day Programme we asked you to select from five goals each of which could be simply monitored. It was merely a question of counting the number of times you smoked a cigarette or ate a slice of bread during the day, or of measuring the amount of time spent doing something. A goal has only been stated correctly if such measurements are possible. For example look at the first goal statement in our inventory: 'I would like to be able to earn more money in my spare time.' It is a fairly simple matter to calculate present earnings and set a realistically desired goal for the amount by which income is to be increased. A series of sub-goals can then be constructed leading to the target. There, measurement is by units of currency. But what about the second goal statement on the list: 'I would like to be able to co-operate better with my marriage partner at home'? Clearly the sub-goals will consist of behaviours in which such co-operation takes place. Possibly helping around the house, going shopping, assisting in working out the family budget. These behaviours can be measured by time or frequency. For example during the preliminary observation and analysis period it might be found that a total of twenty incidents of co-operation involving some five hours of time occurred. The overall goal might then be to increase the incidence of co-operation from twenty to fifty a week or the time involved from five to ten hours. Which form of measurement took place would depend on the kind of programme being implemented.

The point is that all the goal statements in our inventory, because they have been correctly stated, are capable of measurement. Vague ambitions like: 'Being more successful . . . being a better person . . .' are incapable of measurement. If, on the other hand they were stated in this form: 'I would like to gain faster promotion at work' or 'I would like to be more patient and understanding with my family' then they could be broken down into sub-goals and the behaviours involved in attaining each overall goal discovered. As these new behaviours were put into effect it would be possible to measure the ways, and the rate at which, change took place. In the first case an analysis of the work situation might show that it was an inability to prepare and present work effectively, or lack of confidence when dealing with clients that was delaying promotion. The programme to overcome these problems would involve procedures for effective presentation or strategies for gaining confidence. In each case the rate of progress could be measured and the incidence of appropriate or inappropriate behaviour recorded and measured. In the second case the preliminary analysis would pin-point how, when and why disputes within the family occurred in which the lack of patience or understanding showed itself. Suppose it was found that in a week fifteen such incidents occurred. The overall goal would then be to decrease such behaviour to zero. As the programme of behaviour change was carried out the sub-goals, each one a gradual reduction in the number of undesirable interactions, could be recorded and progress towards the overall goal assessed.

2 The goal must be positive

'I wish I wasn't so stupid when it comes to remembering things.'
'I wish I didn't give way so easily when people argue against me.'

Both these goals are incorrectly stated because they express negative ambitions which are usually impossible to measure. Correctly stated they might read as follows:

'I would like to be able to remember facts and figures and recall them quickly in a discussion.'
'I would like to be able to put my viewpoint over forcefully and convincingly when arguing with my husband.'

You will find it quite easy to state goals positively if you start them with the phrase: 'I would like to be able to . . .' This is a better start to a goal statement than: 'I wish . . .' because the other suggests that some kind of magic or luck is involved in achievement. Where realistic goals are concerned fulfilment is a matter of employing the right behavioural programme, not of fate.

Having started with this positive statement of intent: 'I would like to be able to . . .' carry on in the same way by avoiding all negative terms. Don't use words like 'don't'! Avoid words like 'never, not, no, or none'. Use 'more' instead of 'less'. Say: 'I would like to be able to be more tolerant when dealing with employees.' Not: 'I would like to be less impatient when dealing with employees.'

Even if you want to decrease a piece of behaviour state the goal in a positive way. If you want to be less inhibited when making love, turn the phrase around and say: 'I would like to be able to be more passionate when making love.' If you want to play golf with less anxiety don't say you would like to be 'less nervous' but 'more confident'.

3 The goal must be located within some environment or situation

In Part One we explained that behaviour can only be usefully considered in relation to the environment in which it happens. Goals, which can now be seen as pieces of behaviour, must clearly be located in the same way.

'I would like to be able to remember facts and figures *during a meeting with a client.*'

'I would like to be able to be more tolerant when dealing with my *children at home.*'

'I would like to be able to make friends more easily *at a party.*'

At first you may find it easier to write down your goals under two headings:

Goal	Environment
To hold successful parties	At home
To find sex more enjoyable	With my boy-friend
To present my ideas clearly	During meetings with my boss

Here are some case histories which will help to make the three rules of goal specifying clear.

Julia, aged 19, secretary: 'I share a flat with two other girls. It's a great place, or it would be if the others weren't so untidy. Perhaps I'm over-sensitive but I like everything to be neat and clean. We are always having rows about it. They say I am being silly and I suppose they are right to some extent. I wish we could share the flat without rows.'

Incorrectly stated Julia's goal might be: 'I wish I could accept people as they are and not be so fussy.'

Correctly stated it reads: 'I would like to be able to behave more tolerantly in the flat.'

Arthur, aged 66, retired accountant: 'Since my wife died I have been at a loose end. I have plenty of friends, belong to clubs and get out a good deal. I am not lonely but I wish I was more creatively occupied. I started oil painting but couldn't stick at it. I thought of trying to learn a language but that seems too difficult at my age. I am terribly aware of time passing and being wasted.'

Incorrectly stated, Arthur's goal might be: 'I wish I could find something interesting to do.'

Correctly stated it reads: 'I would like to be able to find a creative hobby to do at home.'

Mark, *aged 23*, *engineering draughtsman:* 'Since starting work with a new firm I have felt very lonely. I left my old friends behind when I moved and I have found it hard to make new ones. I have tried going to pubs and dances but people seem very reserved and not willing to make the effort. I try to start a conversation but it never develops into anything worthwhile.'

Incorrectly stated, Mark's goal might be: 'I wish I was less lonely.' Correctly stated it is: 'I would like to be able to make new friends outside my work.'

Specifying goals correctly is a neglected skill, but an easy one to learn. Once you have mastered it you will have carried out the first part of our definition of success – the setting up and attainment of goals.

Sub-goal three – identifying barriers to success

Even with the goal specified correctly attainment may not be as straightforward as it appears. Barriers can arise on the road to success, obstacles which may appear insurmountable when first encountered. They are not, but conquering them demands more than willpower. It requires a knowledge of the psychological factors at work and the procedures for overcoming them. These barriers to success, how and why they arise and how they can be removed will be explained in a moment. Now we would like you to try and identify such barriers in your own life by carrying out the following analysis.

Read through the list of *Attempted behaviour* under the Life Area heading which you identified as having particular significance for you at the moment. Pick out those statements closest to pieces of behaviour which you have attempted to carry out recently. Write them down. Now read through the *Environment* list and select appropriate locations in which the pieces of attempted behaviour took place. Write these down as well. Finally look down the list of *Actual behaviour* and try to find statements which correspond, if only approximately, to the way you responded. Write these down as well so that you have a statement which indicates attempted behaviour in a particular environment which produced a response contrary to what you hoped for or intended.

Life area A – work and study

Attempted behaviour
Holding a meeting with staff.
Making a good impression on a client.
Defending a point with a superior.
Dealing with criticism of work.
Criticising or reprimanding an employee.
Supporting a point of view in a boardroom situation.
Planning an efficient work or study programme.
Holding an office party.
Making my point with a client.

Environment
In my own office.
In a superior's office.
With colleagues or staff in a formal role.
With colleagues or staff in an informal setting.
With clients in my office.
In meeting with superiors.
In meeting with colleagues.
With clients outside or in their own office.

Actual behaviour
I cannot hold the attention of colleagues or staff.
I usually lose in confrontation with boss, even when in the right.
I allow other people's viewpoints to triumph.
I become too stiff and formal.
I become too tense to express myself clearly.
My attention wanders and I procrastinate or day-dream.
No one seems to take any notice of my presence or point of view.
I can never remember the facts and figures clearly in arguments and discussions.
I stammer and blush.
I become extremely tense and my heart races very fast.

I am frightened of holding discussions over the telephone.
I dislike opening letters because they may contain bad news.
I feel I am bound to fail at my task before I start.
I find it impossible to keep order.
I find it impossible to make people respect me.
I find it difficult to criticise or reprimand people.
I am unable to take praise graciously.
I feel insufficiently qualified for the work I do.
I lose interest in my task.
I find it impossible to keep the point in mind.
I am too easily distracted.
I procrastinate.

Life area B – family, marriage, sex and intimacy

Attempted behaviour
Sexual intercourse.
Holding conversation with member of family.
Visiting relatives.
Being visited by relatives.
Playing with children.
Discussing ambitions with partner.
Telling partner about good and bad feelings.
Asserting myself when I have been wronged.
Petting.
Being looked at.

Environment
In a sexually intimate situation.
In a socially relaxing situation with partner.
In an interpersonal situation with partner, i.e. just the two of us alone.
With relatives.
With children at home.
In situations of injustice with partner.
In public places.
In the homes of others.

Actual behaviour

I do not become sexually aroused.

I find it difficult or impossible to get an erection.

I find sex distasteful.

I ejaculate prematurely.

I am not able to complete the act of intercourse satisfactorily.

I find it difficult to talk to my partner.

I feel that my partner and relatives do not understand me.

I think there are too many people visiting me and invading my privacy.

I cannot let myself go in play situations with the children.

I cannot have fun and be irresponsible when it is appropriate.

I cannot disclose my feelings to my partner.

I cannot compliment my partner.

I become convinced that I will fail.

I cannot stand up for my rights against my partner.

I become physically tense and anxious.

I avoid the situation as much as possible.

Life area C – social and interpersonal relationships

Attempted behaviour

Making small talk.

Listening to others.

Addressing an informal group.

Giving a talk.

Discovering areas of common conversational interest.

Breaking the ice with a difficult conversationalist.

Telling people I feel they are wrong.

Telling people of my liking or affection for them.

Standing up against an unjust criticism against myself.

Environment

At an informal party.

In a lecture hall.

At a formal gathering.

In a restaurant.

In a theatre or cinema.

With one person.
In a provocative situation.
In a shop.
In a vehicle.
In a situation of injustice.

Actual behaviour

I find I am tongue-tied and stuck for words.
I become extremely tense and my heart beats rapidly.
My attention wanders.
I cannot stick to my notes or keep my mind on what I am saying.
I stammer.
I blush.
Thoughts rush through my head that I will make a fool of myself.
I am unable to stand up against criticism.
I am unable to express my feelings.
I am unable to assert my rights.
I feel people are looking at me and I become uneasy.
I feel people are criticising me.
I feel I want to run away.
I procrastinate.

Life area D – leisure and sport

Attempted behaviour

Playing an individual sport such as golf or tennis.
Playing a team sport.
Writing, painting, playing musical instruments.
Taking further educational courses.
Planning and developing a new hobby.
Planning for increased leisure time.
Travelling for pleasure.

Environment

In a sports setting.
In a quiet, creative setting.
In a competitive setting.
In retirement.
In an educational setting.

At home.
Under public scrutiny.
In public transport.
In private transport.

Actual behaviour
I have no drive to win.
If I play a bad shot this disrupts my game for several more shots.
I become too tense to perform effectively.
I become convinced that I am going to lose and usually do.
I become overawed by spectators.
I am unable to set myself a timetable of work.
I find it hard to concentrate.
I find it hard to know where to begin.
I find it hard to motivate myself.
I soon lose interest, especially if something does not go right
for me.
I become easily disheartened.
I don't know what to do with my spare time.
I perspire and become tense, my heart races.
I keep telling myself something dreadful will happen.
I avoid certain forms of transport.
I avoid certain things in the situation.

The main rule to be extracted from these necessarily brief lists is
that behaviour must be considered in relation to three variables:

1 The attempted behaviour.
2 The stimulus control (environment and circumstances at the
time).
3 The actual response produced as a result of the interactions of
the first two.

In all these situations the desired behaviour constitutes a goal
to be attained. If, as in the analysis statements, there is a considerable discrepancy between attempted behaviour and actual behaviour then the goal has not been achieved. It has been frustrated
by an inappropriate response. This response, in turn, can be considered as a barrier to success. So long as it remains the desired
goal will not be achieved and frustration will result. The main

objective of a behaviour modification programme is to match the actual behaviour which results to the behaviour attempted so that the discrepancy disappears. Some examples may make this point clear.

1 Goal (desired behaviour)

To persuade business associates to follow a particular course of action.

Appropriate behaviour: Deliver a strong and logical argument in favour of the policy being advocated.

Inappropriate behaviour: Presentation of views in a muddled or half-hearted way. An inability to think clearly on one's feet or to remember key facts and figures. A stammering or hesitant delivery. A feeling of panic which results in an underconfident and unimpressive presentation.

Barrier: Incorrect physical response produces mental confusion.

Solution: Eliminate incorrect physical response by learning

a to relax physically in the negotiation and
b to plan strategies for presenting material coherently and persuasively.

2 Goal

To achieve a good result in an examination.

Appropriate behaviour: Clear and logical presentation of relevant material during examination in answer to carefully selected and fully understood questions.

Inappropriate behaviour: Inability to concentrate during study periods, difficulty in learning material. Extreme anxiety during exam causing incorrect understanding of questions, poor planning, poor use of time allowed. Inability to recall important facts and figures.

Barrier: Stress produces incorrect mental and physical response to circumstances.

Solution: Removal of physical stresses by techniques of relaxation.

Removal of mental stresses by devising a study and revision programme in which both memory and recall of information can be improved, practice in presenting material in logical sequences under time constraints and developing strategies for choosing the examination questions most likely to produce high marks.

3 Goal

To go out on dates with attractive members of the opposite sex and enjoy their company.

Appropriate behaviour: Go to social gatherings or places where such meetings can first take place. Start a conversation which holds their interest.

Inappropriate behaviour: Inability to go to meeting-places or unable to start a conversation. Feeling that others are being critical of looks and behaviour. Too shy to make dates. Feeling of personal inadequacy over looks, manners or clothes.

Barrier: Lack of confidence leading to stress which makes situations even harder to cope with.

Solution: Motivation to make dates by using self-reinforcement to increase frequency of attempts. Learning to make interesting and effective conversation and planning talking points beforehand. Learning to relax differentially in order to remove tension and anxiety while chatting.

4 Goal

To smoke fewer cigarettes each day.

Appropriate behaviour: Gradually to reduce the number smoked.

Inappropriate behaviour: Tension mounts when attempts made to refuse a cigarette. Overwhelming need to smoke in certain situations, for example when driving, under stress, when waiting for something to happen.

Barrier: Stress too great when reduction is attempted.

Solution: Identify periods when most cigarettes smoked. Reinforce behaviour change using behavioural approach. Combat stress with quick relaxation techniques.

From these examples you can see that there are two types of barrier:

1 The effects of physical stress where high levels of bodily tension and anxiety interfere with appropriate speech patterns, writing ability, muscular co-ordination and other physical movements.

2 The effects of mental stress where the absence of a well planned and previously mentally rehearsed set of strategies leads to confusion and inability to think of the appropriate action to take in response to the situation.

Of course these two major barriers, the physical and the mental, are almost always to be seen together. Often the high degree of muscular tension and anxiety will result in our minds going completely blank and rendering us incapable of thinking of a suitable response. In the same way a sudden realisation that we do not know the appropriate way in which to behave or that we have forgotten an important point in the development of our actions may lead to a surge of anxiety and bodily tension. Whichever came first there is, usually, a circular feedback effect between the two areas of stress which spirals into a complete break-down of our ability to respond effectively.

Sub-goal four – understanding how these barriers arise and how they can be removed

Physical barriers

These can arise when attempting a wide range of human activities, from playing in a competitive sport to public speaking; when making love or when trying to make friends. A phobia is an example of a very powerful physical barrier, but they need not be so dramatic to have a very handicapping effect on behaviour. Frequently they seem to strike out of the blue and an individual who has always managed to function effectively will suddenly find themselves flooded with an intense, and frequently alarming fear. In the following three case histories victims of unexpected physical barriers describe what happened to them when this fear struck.

Susan, aged 25, teacher: 'Two months ago I applied for a new teaching post. I was well qualified and they asked me to attend an interview before the school board. I have experience of this type of interview and didn't feel at all anxious until I sat down in front of them. Then, for no good reason, I started to stammer. This is something I never do before a class. I couldn't get my words out. They were patient but this only made matters worse. I started to feel sick and a little faint. I just lost all my confidence. I couldn't answer the simplest question. My heart was racing. I knew I was making a disastrous impression and I couldn't get out of that room fast enough. Now I am haunted by the fear of what will happen if I ever attend another interview. But unless I am able to face a selection board again I will never get another post.'

Brian, aged 24, medical student: 'I knew the subject of my end of term exam well. I had done a lot of studying, really concentrated. But the first question baffled me. This may have been what threw me. I don't know. But I found myself going to pieces. My hand was shaking so badly I could hardly hold the pen. My stomach was churning and my guts cramped agonisingly. I started to sweat. In the end I just had to get out of the damned hall. I wrote down whatever came into my head so that I could finish early and get out of it.'

Alan, aged 30, steel worker: 'Until two years ago I was a virgin. Perhaps that sounds incredible but I had never been very good with girls. I was interested enough but I am a very shy sort of man. My parents were religious and didn't believe you should have sex outside marriage. Eventually I found a girl I liked and we got married. But when we tried to have sex it was a nightmare. I began by feeling very anxious. I started to shiver even in the warm bed. I was trembling. I wanted to make love to her, I did love her, but it was a pretty poor sort of performance. I felt sick before, during and afterwards. I didn't enjoy it and I am sure she didn't either.'

All three are articulate and intelligent. They all wanted to think themselves out of their physical anxiety but they were quite unable to do so. Nor, in a similar situation, is it likely you would have done any better unless you were aware of the psychological and physiological reasons why you felt as you did and knew the correct procedures for banishing the tension.

Think back to the last time you were in a stressful situation. This might have been a near accident in the car, or an encounter with a critical superior. It may have been standing up to speak before a large audience or when arguing your position with a colleague or client. It is possible that you experienced some, or all, these symptoms of stress. Your stomach churned and your mouth went dry. You paled and started to sweat. You felt your heart racing. Perhaps you began to feel faint. You may have started to tremble. You found it hard to express your ideas clearly or forcefully. After the encounter you still felt weak. Your digestion was upset and possibly your head started to throb.

Why should this have happened? What purpose is served by our responding to stress in such an uncomfortable and, apparently, useless manner? To answer these questions we must examine the control systems which link the brain to the rest of the body, and realise that we are basically twentieth-century people operating inside Stone Age machines.

For our prehistoric ancestors life tended to be short, sharp and brutal with stressful encounters centred around wild beasts and homicidal neighbours rather than career struggles and domestic strife. To cope with this situation man evolved two separate nervous systems. One is the *cortical nervous system* and comes under the direct control of the thinking mind. When we are being creative or practical we are using the *cerebral cortex*. The second system takes care of those essential but routine bodily functions which would tie up the thinking mind unnecessarily. This system is called the *autonomic nervous system* and can be likened to the automatic pilot in an aircraft. While our cortex is enabling us to compose music, write books, play tennis, earn a living and bring up a family, the *autonomic nervous system* keeps our hearts beating, our digestion working and our chest and diaphragm muscles operating so that we can breathe. This system has also been called the 'fight or flight' survival mechanism because it is of major importance during emergencies. It is with this system, which does not come under the direct control of the thinking brain, that we are now concerned.

The *autonomic nervous system* has two divisions, the *sympathetic* and the *parasympathetic* branches which work in opposition to one another and, in this way, maintain a balance. The *sympathetic* branch is energy expending. Its function is to speed up the heart, increase the blood pressure, make us breathe more rapidly. The *parasympathetic* branch is energy conserving. Its task is to slow down the heart rate, lower blood pressure and keep us breathing evenly.

Most of the time the energy expending power of the *sympathetic* branch is matched by the energy conserving powers of the *parasympathetic* branch and a state of physical equilibrium exists. We remain cool, calm and collected.

When we come under stress, however, the *sympathetic* branch at once gains mastery, even though this mastery may be fleeting. Designed for Stone Age living the *sympathetic* branch responds as if every situation can only be survived by fighting or fleeing. Which choice is made will depend on the thinking brain. The job of the *sympathetic* branch is to prepare the body, like a battle cruiser sounding action stations, for massive physical effort.

To this end it begins to release glucose from the liver into the blood stream and increase the rate of respiration. At the same time the heart beat increases and blood pressure is stepped up. This ensures that food and oxygen-rich blood are available to those muscles needed for running or fighting. At the same time blood is diverted away from less necessary organs, such as the stomach and skin, so that the maximum amount can be pumped into the brain and muscles. The digestion is slowed down or stopped, the salivary glands no longer produce fluid. Both these activities are unnecessary in a body stripped down to a war economy. In a burst of energy a great deal of heat will be produced, so the *sympathetic* branch increases the rate of sweating and erects body hairs to help cool the system down. It even speeds up the rate at which blood will clot so that damage from wounds can be minimised.

This is all very effective if the body follows such massive arousal by actually fighting or fleeing. The released energy will be burned up and, with the emergency over, the energy conserving *parasympathetic* branch will be able to restore order.

But twentieth-century man fights or runs only rarely. Usually he stands or sits still and absorbs the stress; confronts the critical boss or the angry spouse, remains strapped and trapped in his car as he slides across the wet road; argues eye-ball to eye-ball with the furious customer or inept employee.

As this happens the *parasympathetic* branch may attempt to restore the body to normal running. It slows down the heart, reduces the blood pressure, reinstates digestion and diverts the blood back to the skin. But just as quickly the *sympathetic* branch switches back to emergency running. The threat is still there and the system is programmed to physical survival.

The result is internal confusion on a grand scale. As blood flows to and from the skin the person under stress alternately flushes and pales. Sweat shines on the skin. The heart races. Blood pressure soars dangerously. The mouth feels dry. The stomach churns and cramps as it is ordered to stop and start digestion. The rush of blood from the brain may produce a lightheadedness, or a feeling of fainting. Nausea wells up into the parched mouth. The thinking brain, bewildered by the panic-stricken feedback from the body, becomes confused and uncertain. The memory is clogged. Ideas cease to flow. Uneven breathing and a dry mouth lead to a hesitant and stuttering delivery.

We have all experienced this very unpleasant response at some time in our lives and know how damaging it can be to performance. An excellent example of this inappropriate behaviour in action is the case of Henry, a twenty-two-year-old sales executive who came to see us a few weeks after being sent on a management course. It should have been the first step towards promotion, but when the course was over Henry was very doubtful about his chances. During the course, he explained, each trainee had to complete a project and then report to the other students and the staff on their findings. He had done a first class project and felt very confident of success, a confidence which vanished the moment he rose to speak. This is how he described what happened: 'Even before I stood up I knew that something terrible was going to happen. I had grown increasingly anxious as my turn came closer and closer. I put this down to natural nerves about addressing a large and potentially critical audience, it was the first time I had

had to do any public speaking. But as soon as I got on my feet I was overwhelmed by the most dreadful sense of panic. The violence of my physical reaction horrified me. I tried to tell myself not to be an idiot, but it did no good. My legs trembled violently and my hands holding the notes shook. I thought I was going to faint. I felt all the blood rush to my face. My stomach was churning over and over. The muscles of my neck and jaw tightened and my mouth became bone dry. When I finally managed to stutter a few words they sounded like an audition for the part of Donald Duck. Everybody was very kind about this terrible disaster but I felt depressed and humiliated. Soon the anxiety spread over into other areas of my life. From being confident I started to wonder about my abilities and doubted that I could ever pass the course. I felt I could never succeed in a job which demanded any type of public speaking.'

It is, of course, perfectly normal to feel some anxiety when confronted by a challenging situation. In small and manageable doses it even helps because it keys-up the system and improves performance. But when the response is as violent as in the examples outlined such behaviour is quite inappropriate and handicapping. Not only does it prevent us from operating efficiently at the moment it happens but the halo effect causes a general loss of confidence. After his first, disastrous examination Brian began seriously to doubt his suitability for a university career. Alan whose first attempts at intercourse were so unfortunate told us that he not only fought shy of having intercourse but even became underconfident in his relations with his wife.

It is not even necessary to be confronted by an external threat for the *autonomic nervous system* to take control. We can think ourselves into a state of arousal quite easily. Using a piece of monitoring equipment known as a galvanic skin response (GSR) meter we can demonstrate this self-induced arousal very simply. The subject sits in a comfortable chair with electrodes attached to two fingers. These will monitor small changes in the rate of perspiration by measuring the electrical conductance of the skin.

The subject is asked to relax. As he does so the rate of perspiration decreases and the GSR meter registers the drop. Now the subject is asked to imagine driving a car. Immediately the needle on the meter moves up the scale. The *sympathetic* branch, responding to the idea of being in a potentially dangerous environment, is starting to arouse the body. But the degree of arousal is very slight and the *parasympathetic* branch swiftly brings the situation back to normal. The GSR meter shows a decrease in sweating. Now we tell the subject he is in a car at night. It is raining hard and the road is slippery. The GSR needle moves sharply upwards as the subject becomes aroused by the *sympathetic* branch. We tell him that he is sliding into a corner. The car is out of control. Suddenly the lights of a truck flash across the screen. A serious accident is inevitable. The GSR needle flicks almost off the scale. The subject is very aroused, his body keyed-up for survival. But if you then ask him: 'Were you nervous? Did you feel the anxiety your body was registering?' he may say 'no' and even that he felt calm. He knew it was only imagination. His thinking mind was not disturbed in the slightest by the accident fantasy. But his body was highly aroused.

This simple experiment illustrates two important points. Firstly, that we may be physically aroused and anxious without being aware of the fact. Secondly, that while we can think ourselves into a state of arousal we are not able to think ourselves out of it. Like the crew of an aircraft with the automatic pilot engaged we are helpless – until we learn how to switch off the robot and take command of the machine. The lever that gives us this control is relaxation.

When we relax we put our bodies into a deep state of *parasympathetic* arousal. Under these circumstances the power of the *sympathetic* branch to switch on to emergency running is curtailed. We may still feel a little tension and anxiety. This may not be undesirable. Often, a small amount of arousal may key us up and in this sense it is true to say that the secret of success is not to banish but to manage. To exert control over every aspect of our behaviour at all times and even make use of low levels of anxiety.

Mental barriers
These occur when the thinking mind responds to particular situations with negative thoughts, negative expectations or confusion over which course of action to take. In general they are character-

ised by the absence of any well formulated plan of action or set of strategies which might help the person through the situation which has been encountered. The following examples may make this type of behaviour clear:

Anne, aged 20, student nurse: 'So far I have failed my driving test three times. In practice sessions I am perfect. But when it comes to the test I just know I am going to fail. I get into the car with a terrible feeling of doom. I have failed before and I will fail again. I get flustered and make silly mistakes. I have absolutely no confidence although I do feel I am a perfectly competent driver at other times.'

Carl, aged 35, accountant: 'I can get on well with most of my clients but one man scares the life out of me. Unfortunately he is a very important client and I can't afford to tell him to go to hell. Yet every time we have a meeting I find myself turning into a witless "yes" man. Even with points which I regard as vital I can't argue against him. He's an idiot over some things but he is so confident and dominant that I can't ride over him. I don't seem to have any willpower where he is concerned.'

Diana, aged 32, housewife: 'My husband is very assertive and has firm opinions on some things. He was brought up by a strict father and believes that our children should be physically punished if they do something wrong. I completely disagree with him but I can never stop him from beating them. We have rows about it, but he does most of the talking. I try to argue against him but I'm no good at it. I am very unhappy about the situation because I think he is turning the boys against us. I want to stand up and fight him over this but I'm defeated before I start as I can never think of the right things to say at the time.'

None of these people talks about an inappropriate physical reaction. Each saw the problem as a mental one, of not being able to think quickly and effectively when the situation demanded it. They all felt they were beaten before they started and such prophesies of failure are almost always correct!

But why should this happen? As we said in the section on physical barriers, the second important control mechanism in the central nervous system is that of the *cerebral cortex*. This is the part of the brain which integrates all the information which we take in through our senses and allows us to interpret what our environment is doing to us. It then sends signals to our muscles and speech centres, so enabling us to speak and move in response to our surroundings. In many cases the signals sent out by the *cerebral cortex* are transmitted extremely rapidly because the type of situation to which we are now responding is one which has been experienced and dealt with many times in the past. For example when taking avoiding action in a car or when making a move in a game or sport our reactions are very fast because we have learned the rules very thoroughly through experience and laid down guidelines for coping. However, in novel situations or situations where we are not very practised our responses may be considerably slower as our *cerebral cortex* does not have any guidelines by which to direct our actions.

These guidelines or short-cuts by which the *cerebral cortex* makes its decisions to act and send out signals comprise the *strategies* of the *cortex*. Essentially the *cortex* consists of a processing unit which takes in information from the outside world, feeds it through a set of already previously learned *strategies* which give it several options of what to do with the information and then, depending upon the way in which the *strategies* have processed the information, send out signals for speech or body movement.

The situation can be likened to a motorist driving from one town to the next. If he has done the journey before and knows the various routes to follow he is equipped with a set of such *strategies*. Then, when he is given the task of travelling from one town to the next at a certain time of day against a deadline, he can decide on which route to take by considering which *strategy* will be most appropriate. He may consider, for example, that a slightly longer route around the minor roads is preferable due to rush hour congestion on the main highway. Without this prior knowledge of the road conditions he is likely to encounter and the *strategies* which allow the best route, he would be forced to pick his way at random and endure a series of set-backs along the road.

This simple explanation of what is, in fact, the most complex piece of machinery in our bodies enables us to understand how mental stress and confusion might arise. If a person has had prior knowledge and experience with certain patterns and types of behaviour he will have built up sets of *strategies* for these situations over a period of time. Then, when he is faced with similar problems, he has guidelines by which he can move quite quickly to a solution. For instance, a politician who has become practised at dealing with heckling and abuse by his opponents will usually be able to put his point strongly without being distracted or particularly upset. He has learned that there are *strategies* for dealing with this type of behaviour from his environment and makes his speech patterns effective to deal with it. On the other hand, a person who has generally tended to avoid certain sorts of situation for one reason or another during his life, will not have built up any *coping strategies* should such situations arise. For example a young woman who has always felt it best to avoid any confrontations or arguments during her childhood and adolescence may be completely overawed and unable to cope with a domineering office manageress when she begins work.

Just as the ability to control the *sympathetic* branch of the *autonomic nervous system* was of major importance in dealing with physical stress, so the development of *coping strategies* is essential for dealing with mental stress.

Mental and physical barriers

It is rare for either a mental or a physical barrier to arise entirely in isolation. Usually physical tension produces mental confusion, and negative thinking results in anxiety which creates bodily tension.

Why does one respond in this way?

By now the answer should be clear to you. A barrier, whether mental or physical, is a piece of inappropriate behaviour and, like all behaviours exists because it has been learned.

The therapy of the behavioural psychologist involves identifying such pieces of behaviour and replacing them with responses which will lead to fulfilment rather than frustration of goals. For the purposes of making the mechanism of such learning clear, it may be useful to look again at the case of Henry, the sales executive who discovered that he was unable to speak in public. A short course of therapy, it lasted no more than a fortnight, was enough to replace his inappropriate behaviour with the ability to speak clearly, confidently and effectively before any size of audience. And during treatment an explanation of how the problem arose emerged.

As a teenager Henry was very good at history. He was regarded by the master as a star pupil and expected to produce above average work. Each week the boys had to prepare a short talk and a few of them were told to deliver it to the rest of the class. Henry, the favourite, was usually one of the pupils selected. He enjoyed this and was good at it.

One afternoon he felt off colour. There was an outbreak of flu at the school and he was going down with it. Unfortunately so was the master, who felt irritable and more than usually critical. Because he had not felt well the night before, Henry had failed to prepare his talk properly. He made a poor showing and the master was disappointed. Henry was criticised and felt humiliated. The other boys, no doubt delighted by this fall from grace, responded by sniggering. Henry's body went into sympathetic arousal. He began to feel sick. He blushed and started to sweat. His heart pounded.

If the matter had ended there perhaps little harm would have been done. But on the next occasion the master, perhaps still angry at being let down, remained critical. The week after, Henry did a particularly good piece of work and waited, anxiously, to win back the master's esteem. But he was not asked to speak and so, in our terms, received no positive reinforcement for his efforts. The following week Henry felt ill and missed the history class. In doing so he experienced an overwhelming sense of relief which could, of course, be seen as negative reinforcement for missing the class. The following week he found another excuse for not going to the class. Again the feeling of relief was tremendous and further negative reinforcement occurred and the avoidance strengthened.

With this progressive withdrawal from participation in talking in front of the class came the increasing conviction that he would not be able to deliver another essay and the gradual dwindling, through disuse, of those *strategies* he had previously learned for doing so. These included speaking clearly, confidently and with a good volume, maintaining good eye contact with the other boys in the class, and remaining calm and collected when he was asked questions about the work afterwards. Now the subject, once looked on with pleasure, was a focus for his anxieties. When he was forced to speak he became tongue-tied and nervous, responding physically and mentally in a completely negative way. This learned negativeness reasserted itself years later when he again rose to speak before an audience.

In summary we can describe the physical and mental barriers as follows:

Physical barriers = lack of control over the sympathetic branch of the autonomic nervous system.
Procedure for overcoming physical barriers = relaxation methods used in stressful circumstances to control tension effects of the sympathetic branch.
Mental barriers = lack of strategies programmed into the cerebral cortex.
Procedure for overcoming mental barriers = establishing strategies for decision making and behaviour by the use of structured learning programmes.

Sub-goal five – understanding how to carry out a detailed self-analysis

The time has now come to write the most important part of this book – and you are going to have to do the writing! Only *you* have access to the information needed to produce an accurate analysis of your behaviour in relation to your chosen goal.

During the Fourteen-Day Programme you gained experience in recording *baseline data* in relation to one of five goals. This was fairly simple data as the goals themselves involved easily monitored pieces of behaviour. It may be that collecting data during the next seven days will prove no more complicated, or it could be much more involved. This depends on the type of goal you have chosen.

The first step is to state your goal correctly. Write it down and remember to make it specific and positive and to locate it in a particular situation or environment.

Record keeping

This is a Seven-Day Programme, but it may not necessarily be a seven *consecutive* day programme. It will depend on the frequency with which you perform the behaviour under investigation. For example suppose that your goal is to play a better game of golf by learning to surmount early tension and missed shots. If you only play golf once or twice a week it may be necessary to extend the monitoring over the period it takes to play three or four games. It is only necessary to record seven *separate* examples of stress causing missed opportunities and bungled shots, although you would not be advised merely to record seven examples from a single game should these occur. What you are after is a good, overall view of your behaviour, not related to feelings on any specific day. We have chosen seven days as a practical monitoring period; long enough to gather a satisfactory amount of baseline data, but not so long that the task becomes tedious.

How to gather baseline data

1 Make the day to day records on scraps of paper, small pieces of card, or a pocket recorder as you did during the Fourteen-Day Programme. Transfer all the information to your monitoring charts each evening.

2 Be careful that you do not attempt to alter your behaviour as you monitor it. This may be difficult because you will gain insights that reveal just how inappropriate certain of your responses are. But you *must* resist the temptation for change during the analysis period. Remain objective. Observe and record only.

3 Make certain that you jot down all the necessary information at the time. Do not rely on memory. You may believe that you have actually recalled what happened when you have only remembered what you *wanted* to.

4 If you ask your friends to help by pointing out certain pieces of behaviour then be sure they are willing and able to do this in a

neutral manner. If they say: 'You just did . . .' that is helpful. If they add some sarcastic comment they will be introducing a punishing and harmful element into the analysis.

5 As during the Fourteen-Day Programme you will be recording information under the headings of *Stimulus: Response: Consequence.* In addition we would like you to note under a fourth heading the ways in which you would like to have behaved.

Stimulus
The success of the behaviour modification programme will depend to a great extent on the accuracy and consistency with which you have noted down all possible details of the surroundings in which a piece of behaviour takes place. No fact, however apparently trivial, should be overlooked. Remember the case of the woman whose uneasy relationship with her son and daughter-in-law stemmed from her being mildly phobic of cats, and the student who discovered that his problems of concentration were the result of a pile of books. When completed, this column in the analysis chart should enable you to answer the following ten questions about a piece of behaviour:

1 Is it specific to work, social life, the house or in leisure pursuits?
2 Does it happen while travelling?
3 Does it happen when you are in a particular mood or frame of mind?
4 Is there any unusual stress or pressure present when it occurs?
5 Does it happen when people are making demands on you?
6 What time of the day or night does it most frequently occur?
7 On which day or days of the week or times of the year does it most frequently occur?
8 Which sorts of people are present when it occurs? For example, colleagues, superiors, subordinates, clients, family, children, strangers, girl or boy friend?
9 What sorts of objects are usually present when it occurs?
10 Are any animals present regularly when it occurs?

Response
It is important to note down *exactly* which pieces of behaviour on your part cause difficulties. A common mistake when filling in this

section is to be too brief and unspecific about the difficulties encountered. For example, *golfer*:

Environment	Behaviour
Starting round. Weather fine. 11 o'clock. Feeling slightly nervous because crowd watching. Wind making play tricky.	Missed first shots. Play went to pieces. Got angry and had row with spectators.

or, *student*:

Environment	Behaviour
Lecture room. Tutor present and six students. Mid-morning period. Tutor in critical mood. Writing on Roman influence on British cultural traditions. Working with reference books. Dead silence in room. Light good.	Unable to concentrate. Cannot find the points I want. Getting tense and nervous as I watch clock. Writing very poor, hardly legible.

In the first example the golfer should have recorded exactly which shots cause the most trouble. The student should have noted the amount of time available and whether the essay was long or short. It could have been that his poor hand-writing occurred only under a combination of long essays and limited time.

Consequence
It is important that you try and assess the effects of your behaviour on your environment. What was the response of people present? Did they become angry or sarcastic? Were they impressed or depressed? Did they laugh and poke fun at you? How did this influence the way you felt? Did it diminish or increase your confidence? Did you find the consequence rewarding or punishing?

What you would like to have done
Would you have sooner spoken up for yourself in a situation where you were being criticised but remained silent? Would you have preferred to respond to a request for help with enthusiasm and interest rather than an irritable retort?

Note your desired behaviour as carefully and completely as the other information.

Now we would like you to prepare for the first day of analysis. When you start remember these six rules for success.

1 Record behaviour as and when it occurs. Do not rely on memory.
2 Record as much detail as possible – even if some of it seems trivial.
3 Make no attempt to change your behaviour during the analysis period.
4 If you get friends to help they must do so in a neutral manner.
5 Record at least seven examples of behaviour being monitored, whether this takes a week or longer to achieve.
6 Be specific. Vague entries are useless as baseline data.

Detailed examples which illustrate the above rules may be found in Part Five where we explain how to attain major goals in each of the four life areas. If you find that you need to refer to examples at this stage we suggest that you turn to Part Five and read the one under the appropriate life area.

Now make up your charts ready to begin your analysis programme first thing tomorrow or on the first practical occasion.

This ends Day One of the Self-Analysis Programme.

Days two to eight

During this seven-day period you should be recording your baseline data as you learned during the Fourteen-Day Programme. If you run into difficulties at any stage, immediately refer back to this programme in order to clarify any points which may interfere with your record keeping. At the end of the analysis period study your monitoring charts carefully. They should present you with a clear pattern of the stimuli which produce the inappropriate behaviour which, in turn, stands between you and the attainment of the goal which you have set. In Part Four we will show you how to programme your potential in order to remove these barriers to goal attainment and so achieve success.

Part four

Change for the better

In this part of the book we will be describing the basic rules by
which you may construct your own personal programme of
change. We shall discuss the problems which may arise during the
programme and the ways in which you can motivate yourself
through them.

   Examples from actual case histories will be given to show how
these dynamic behavioural change methods can be made to work
quickly and efficiently.

There are five major elements in the achievement of a goal.

1 Realistic aspiration.
2 Realistic appraisal of the situation.
3 Effective motivation.
4 Continuity of effort.
5 The ability to overcome set-backs.

Realistic aspiration

Goals can only be achieved if they lie within your spectrum of potential in the first place. This does not imply however that you should under-estimate your abilities. Many people are capable of achievements which they never even dream of. The secret is to possess sufficient objective insight into your abilities to know which goals lie within your grasp. Never be afraid to try to aim high. Fulfilment can often lie in attempting something really challenging as much as in attaining it. A person who sets out to climb a mountain may learn a great deal about him- or herself and so gain valuable experience in the attempt. Being realistic does not mean being negative in your approach to life – quite the opposite. It means living in the world of potential attainment rather than in a never-never land of fantasy.

Realistic appraisal of the situation

You have achieved this during the seven-day analysis, which will have provided insight into your current behaviour and shown you how this may be inappropriate to your goal.

Effective motivation

Motivation is a word often used loosely and incorrectly to describe a desire to achieve a goal or an inability to do so. 'I suppose I'm just not sufficiently motivated to study,' says a drop-out student. 'I think I am really motivated to do well in this job' claims an enthusiastic young executive.

Motivation can more accurately be described as the following of a piece of behaviour by a reinforcer. You can increase your motivation towards achieving an overall goal in two ways:

A. By correctly structuring a series of sub-goals towards the overall goal in order to ensure that you fail as infrequently as possible (a negative consequence reduces interest in any piece of behaviour which it follows).

B. By using reinforcers.

A. You are less likely to fail when following a correctly graded programme of change than when striking out haphazardly on your own. This is because by giving thought to the sub-goals, you should have been able to space them a comfortable distance apart. Remember that during the Fourteen-Day Programme we asked you to increase or decrease the target behaviour slowly but surely. To cut down by two or three cigarettes per day instead of trying to jump from being a heavy smoker to a light smoker overnight. You climb a mountain foot by foot. You make certain then that every step is manageable. It is the same with goal attainment. You break down a complex piece of behaviour into easy stages. The spacing must be sufficiently wide for you to make clear progress, otherwise you will lose interest in the programme, but not so great that you have to jump ahead instead of walk from step to step.

B. There are three types of reinforcer for behaviour and you have experienced all of them in the earlier programme.

(i) There is a reward which comes from simply achieving the sub-goal. Pride in completing a well presented piece of work, from expressing your arguments so clearly and effectively that you win a point, from going out and meeting people or from other completed sub-goals.

(ii) There can be a reward in the praise of others. This may arise spontaneously, as friends or family congratulate you on some minor, but important achievement. Alternatively it can happen because the people around you are aware that you are trying to modify your behaviour and want to help you. You can also reinforce yourself by thinking positively about your changes in behaviour and by congratulating yourself on the advances made. This brings us to the point that you should never feed yourself negative attitudes and ideas. Avoid saying: 'I can't possibly manage that . . .' or 'I made a complete fool of myself over that . . .' Say instead: 'It certainly is a daunting task. But I have accomplished things which were just as complex and difficult in the past and I see no reason why I can't manage the job.' Tell yourself: 'I didn't behave as I wanted in that situation. But I was able to express some of the ideas in my mind and I think I scored a few important points.'

Remember that we are a part of our own environment!

(iii) The reinforcer can be a tangible reward. This was the main system used during the Fourteen-Day Programme. Remember that the reward must follow close on the behaviour it is being used to establish. There is no point in selecting large rewards which have to be postponed for hours or days after the event. Bear in mind the technique of awarding yourself points which will allow you to 'purchase' some major reward.

Finally, never compare the attainment of a sub-goal with the distance you have to travel to achieve your major goal – or you may become discouraged. If you want to learn a language it is unwise to think of the thousands of words and constructional techniques which will have to be absorbed in the long term. You will probably get discouraged. A practical sub-goal might be to learn ten new words each day. Compared with the total number of words in any language this is a drop in the linguistic ocean, but it soon mounts up. After six months of this type of programme, for example, you would have mastered some 1,680 words. So the technique is to establish the overall goal, structure a pathway of sub-goals to it and then push the ultimate target to the back of your mind. Relate your progress *only* to sub-goals attained and use reinforcers to help you reach each sub-goal in turn.

Continuity of effort

As we explained in Part One any behaviour which is neglected becomes harder to perform. You must be prepared to work *regularly* at a programme of behaviour change. There is no need to devote a vast amount of time each day to it, but try not to let a single day pass without taking a positive step towards your next sub-goal. For change to take place commitment to that change is essential.

The ability to overcome set-backs

Disappointments in life are inevitable and so are set-backs in any programme of behaviour modification, however carefully structured. When they occur you can control them or let them control you. You can turn them to your advantage or you can sit back and let them discourage you from trying any further. When a writer starts out he or she can be certain of one thing: that the bulk of their work is going to be rejected. When this happens the frustrated authors may respond in a variety of ways. They can become so dispirited that they give up and look for other ways of earning a living. Or they may become arrogant, dismiss all editors as mindless, imperceptive ingrates who are unable to realise talent when they see it. Both responses are inappropriate if the goal is to become a professional writer. The appropriate response is to profit from rejections. To find out, usually by learning to appraise work objectively, exactly why it was rejected. Was the writing too poor, or was it wrong for that particular market? Was it too long or too short for the editorial requirements of that magazine? Was the story too sexy or not sexy enough, too slow or too fast? If viewed and used correctly, rejection slips, although they will never cease to disappoint, can be extremely valuable. The same can be said for any set-backs in life. A man rebuffed by a girl may crawl away smarting and decide that women simply are not worth the effort. A more appropriate response would be to try and work out why the girl behaved as she did.

The salesman who fails to pick up orders might blame the goods he had to sell or the people he had to sell them to. Neither response is likely to improve his sales record. The appropriate behaviour is to examine the reason for each and every failure to sell and discover how and why they occurred. To ask if the approach was too high powered, or not positive enough. To discover if the presentation is actually bringing out the key selling points of the product.

Be prepared for set-backs. They are going to happen to you

whichever programme you try to put into effect, whatever goals you have chosen. Learn to use them as a form of behavioural judo, turning the force of disappointment to your own advantage.

Some practical examples

In Part Three we discussed the case of Henry, the executive who found difficulty speaking in public. We also said that two weeks of behavioural therapy was sufficient to turn him into a confident and able public speaker. To illustrate the six elements of goal achievement we will return to this case and outline the treatment used.

His overall goal was to be able to speak fluently without the physical barriers which had thwarted his first attempt during the training course.

This goal could be expressed as follows:
'I would like to be able to talk confidently and interestingly on a difficult technical subject to a large audience of professional people.'

Let us start by dissecting that goal to see if it fulfils all the rules of goal stating.

1 Is it positive? Yes
2 Is it specific? Yes
3 Is it located within a situation/environment setting? Yes

Henry knows when and where he will need to speak effectively.

Finally is it realistic? At the time he came to see us, Henry would probably have answered no to that question. He was quite convinced that his overwhelming physical response was too powerful for him ever to speak fluently before a large audience. But, objectively, he had to admit that the goal was a realistic one. He knew his subject and he had no handicap which might have prevented him from speaking loudly enough and clearly enough to be understood.

Henry was motivated to make the change because he knew that to be able to speak in public would lead to promotion, more money and greater job satisfaction.

The first task was to establish the sub-goals.

1 He had to overcome the problem of tension by learning to relax.
Sub-goal one – Deep relaxation/quick relaxation/differential relaxation.

2 Secondly he had to learn the strategies of public speaking. The first rule is never to try and read a speech. It sounds flat and predictable.
Sub-goal two – To deliver a speech from skeleton notes in order to maintain an interesting and flexible approach.

3 Thirdly he had to learn how to project his voice and vary the pitch, so as to underscore the words by his intonations.
Sub-goal three – To learn effective delivery and tone and volume control.

4 The fourth step was to gain confidence by talking to a small audience.
Sub-goal four – Get used to speaking in front of two or three people.

5 The fifth stage was to gain confidence in talking to a larger and potentially more hostile audience.
Sub-goal five – To get used to speaking to a realistic audience.

6 The final step was the overall goal itself, delivering a complicated technical speech ably.

With the five sub-goals clearly set down he began to practise the necessary skills. While learning to relax he also trained himself to construct a speech from a few main headings jotted down on a piece of card, a prompt sheet small enough to be held in the palm of one hand. He practised this alone, in front of a mirror. At this point he was told to concentrate only on expanding a few lines of notes into a speech lasting several minutes. He did not concern himself with pace, intonation or clarity, as these were to be tackled in Sub-Goal Three. At the end of each session Henry reinforced his behaviour with a reward.

When he had gained confidence in constructing a talk from notes, he moved on to the third sub-goal and using a tape-recorder began to improve pace and delivery. He was still performing for an audience of just one – his own reflection in the mirror. By now he felt confident and eager to test himself before an audience. He might have gone out of his way to find the real thing at work, opportunities were constantly occurring for members of his department to give lectures to different groups. But to have attempted such an ambitious move could have been a disaster. If he had failed again it might have seriously damaged his newly found assurance. So he stuck to his programme and moved to Sub-Goal Four. His family provided a small and friendly audience and he was able to deliver a short talk to them without effort or stress.

He then moved on to Sub-Goal Five when the chance arose to talk to a group of neighbours about a local conservation project. Just before he rose to speak Henry felt extremely nervous, but he was able to cope with the anxiety by using quick relaxation. While standing and speaking he used differential relaxation to remain calm and in control of his tension. A few days later he attained his overall goal by delivering a short but fluent speech to a group of management executives at work.

Perhaps that case seemed rather simpler than most because Henry's goal was so easily specified. You may feel that where deep human emotions are concerned the behaviours involved are too complicated to yield to this precise approach.

Well, there can be few things more sensitive or complex than sexual and marital problems, so let us examine another case from the files. This was a man in his early twenties who was experiencing difficulties in having intercourse with his wife. He was ejaculating prematurely and she was getting very little satisfaction from their love-making. He was starting to lose confidence in his ability and this was making him miserable and nervous. An analysis of the problem showed that they attempted to make love about four times a week and that on the majority of occasions he felt tired, tense and preoccupied by thoughts of failure before and during intercourse. The sub-goals in his behaviour modification programme were as follows:

1 Relaxation training to overcome tension.
2 A reduction in the pace at which he worked during the day.
3 Spending more time with his wife in general to help re-establish the deep affection between them.
4 Learning to relax with his wife while petting, clothed.

5 Learning to remain relaxed when in bed with his wife.
6 Relaxed with his wife with them both naked and caressing one another, although avoiding any genital contact.
7 The use of a more comfortable and easier position during intercourse. (Full details of this programme can be found in Part Five under the Life area of family and marriage.)
8 Introducing movement and thrusting with resting periods.
9 Full coitus without anxiety.

This programme required help and understanding from his wife which was forthcoming. It took some four weeks to work through the sub-goals but, at the end of that time not only was the problem of premature ejaculation overcome but they both reported a deepening of the bond of love. By improving their sexual relationship the programme's 'halo effect' helped to improve their whole marriage and the man's general confidence.

Sometimes we do not even attempt to make changes in our lives because the behaviours involved seem so complex and the dissatisfactions so vague. These difficulties are always more apparent than real. There are no problems too complicated to be broken down into separate pieces of behaviour, behaviour which is appropriate when it leads to the fulfilment of a goal and inappropriate when it leads to the frustration of that goal.

The following case histories should serve to make this clear.

Susan, aged 24, married with a daughter of six months. Her husband is an accountant. Her parents both died when she was a child.
The problem: An increasing number of rows with her husband began to damage Susan's previously happy marriage and led to her feeling tense and depressed. Most of the arguments seemed to take place during the weekends and she grew to dread them. Before starting a programme of self-analysis she had no real idea how her arguments started, but the problem clearly arose in Life area B – *family, marriage, sex and intimacy.*
The analysis: A preliminary analysis using the Barrier Identification Guide suggested to Susan that most of the rows occurred just prior to, or during visits from, Michael's parents who had recently moved to the neighbourhood and were frequent visitors. To investigate this possibility Susan decided to keep a close check

on her behaviour and the behaviour of the others present both before, during and after a visit. As such visits occurred about six times a month, she made the self-analysis period cover seven separate visits rather than merely seven days.

The assessment: By studying the charts at the end of this time, Susan saw clearly how her rows with Michael all centred around her behaviour immediately prior to and sometimes during these visits. Always a perfectionist so far as keeping the house tidy was concerned, Susan became fanatical before a visit. The slightest thing out of place, the smallest scrap of dirt, the thought of something not tidied away was enough to make her irritable and critical of her family. Before the analysis she had looked on this as a perfectly normal desire to have the house look its best. Now she realised she was terrified of criticism from her mother-in-law whom she felt, wrongly as she now realised, would look down on her unless the house was immaculate. This attitude led to tension and provoked the rows.

The programme: From the analysis charts Susan was able to identify ten separate pieces of 'house proud' behaviour related to her concern over criticism from her mother-in-law. She also realised how tense she became before and during a visit and how this caused her to act out of character. Her overall goal was stated as follows:

'I would like to be able to regard visits from my mother-in-law as ordinary and agreeable meetings with a friend.'

Her first sub-goal was to learn relaxation in order to overcome physical tension. Then, in eight further sub-goals she learned to tidy the house normally, but not go through any cleaning purges just prior to a visit. She also taught herself not to criticise her husband for small pieces of behaviour which disturbed the neatness of the house prior to a visit. The overall goal was achieved within two months of starting the programme.

Peter, aged 37, a personnel executive. He is married with two children, a teenage boy and girl.
The problem: Things started to go wrong soon after his company was taken over and a new director, a younger man, appointed to his department. He became increasingly ineffective at work and

105

irritable at home. He started to sleep badly and this led to feelings of depression. During a period of absence through sickness the director made changes in his department which angered him and led to a major row. This he felt, made his whole future with the company uncertain. Anxious about his career he started to drink heavily. His relationship with his wife and children hit rock bottom. At one stage she left home for a few weeks, and his son and daughter stayed out of his way as much as possible. The stress, alcohol and lack of sleep led to a minor heart attack. In hospital he was given sedatives which allowed him to sleep soundly for the first time in months. This rest helped him to take a more objective view of his life and he was persuaded to attempt an analysis of his problems. Initially he felt this would be impossible because there seemed to be so many covering such a wide area of his life. His work, family environment, and social relationships were all involved.

The analysis: As the work and home situations were clearly the most critical, Peter was encouraged to record baseline data about his arguments in both environments. Because these outbursts were so frequent a week proved long enough to gather sufficient information, and gain valuable insights.

The assessment: Peter discovered that most of his rows at home concerned the behaviour of his children. He was either arguing with them, or complaining to his wife about their conduct. At work his arguments centred around decisions made by the new director. He found that in these heated discussions he was always complaining that his experience was being discounted or that things had been better organised prior to the take-over.

The programme: Peter constructed a behaviour modification programme for himself aimed at reducing tension at home and in the office. He set himself two goals: firstly to replace sarcastic and critical comments by constructive or affectionate remarks; and secondly, to limit the number of times when he objected to other people's proposals. When he felt compelled to object he tried to construct logical arguments rather than oppose them with bitter tirades.

Within a month this modified behaviour had reduced tension both at work and at home. All his personal interactions, between his colleagues and superiors, between his wife and his family, changed with his modified behaviour. This had the effect of making him less anxious, less tense and much less irritable.

At the same time he decided to take up a leisure pursuit, something he had always persuaded himself he had no time for, and began to play golf. As he had convinced himself that he would never get further promotion he transferred a lot of the energy which he had been pouring into work into his sport. His health improved with the exercise. He was asked to sit on the golf club committee. The sense of being valued and useful improved his self-image. This improvement in mental and physical health made him work far more effectively. Although he put in less hours than before, he actually got through his work load quicker and made more productive decisions. This led to the promotion which Peter had thought was out of the question.

By now you have probably got a good grasp of the principles of behaviour change. But before attempting to plan your own programme you may find it useful to read some sections of Part Five, where we deal with the most frequently encountered problems in the four life areas.

Summary

If you do want to begin the programme immediately this summary of the procedures should help you achieve the desired results within the shortest possible time. Remember:
Success = the setting up and attainment of goals

Goals

Must be realistic.
Must be stated positively.
Must be specific.
Must be located within a situation or environment.

Programmes

Must be based on accurate *baseline data* collected during a period of observation of behaviour in which no attempt is made to change the behaviour being monitored.

Must be structured through a series of sub-goals which should be so spaced that you can move from one to another with a high probability of success, as failure may cause loss of motivation.

Motivation

May be increased by using systems of positive or negative reinforcement. Reinforcers can be satisfaction in reaching the sub-goal effectively, praise – including self-praise, or an actual external reward. Rewards can be quite minor or major pleasures. The crucial thing is that they immediately follow the piece of behaviour being learned. Do not be shy about using any of your pleasurable activities as reinforcers. Remember that sexual activities of all sorts can be valid reinforcers and may be included in your list. Avoid negative thoughts. Remember that you are part of your own environment and influence it.

Maintain a continuity of effort. Remember that every piece of behaviour becomes more difficult to perform if neglected.

When set-backs occur use them to gain experience. Work from sub-goal to sub-goal and judge achievement on whether you have attained the next step in your programme, not on how close you have come to the overall goal.

Physical and mental barriers

When *physical barriers* occur use relaxation to remove tension and reduce anxiety to a controlled level. Learn how to regulate the effects of your *autonomic nervous system*.

When *mental barriers* of confusion and uncertainty arise develop strategies which will give your *cerebral cortex* an effective route towards the desired goal. Examples of such strategies in each of the four life areas will be found in the next part of this book.

Within the context of behaviour change there is no such thing as good or bad behaviour. There is only appropriate behaviour which leads to the attainment of goals and inappropriate behaviour which prevents the attainment of goals.

Part five

The real you in action

In the first four parts of this book we have explained how to acquire the skills by which you can analyse and modify your behaviour. In Part Five you will find detailed descriptions of how to achieve specific goals in the four life areas. In each of the life areas three goals have been selected which have been found, in our experience, to represent common areas of difficulty.

Four procedures are needed to attain these twelve major goals:

1 Identifying areas of difficulty.

2 Learning the skills and strategies necessary to overcome physical and mental barriers to goal attainment.

3 Learning crisis tactics which can be used when there is too little time for a full behaviour modification programme.

4 Learning to develop a long-term behaviour modification programme which will result in lasting improvements in any of the life areas.

The skills and strategies in each of the life areas should be regarded as building blocks out of which you can construct any programme of behaviour change no matter what your personal goal in life.

In the event that your own particular goal is not specifically included in one of the twelve detailed, proceed as follows:

1 Decide into which of the four life areas your own goal fits.

2 Go through the list of statements in that life area and complete those which can be made applicable to your particular aims.

3 Use your answers to guide you to the physical skills and mental strategies listed in that life area.

4 From these extract those which, perhaps with some slight changes, can be made applicable to your own behaviour modification programme.

The following frequently expressed goals will be covered in this part of the book.

Life area A – work and study

'I would like to be able to . . .
1 achieve better examination results' (p 112)
2 create the best impression during interviews' (p 122)
3 gain faster promotion at work' (p 132)

Life area B – family, marriage, sex and intimacy

'I would like to be able to . . .
1 enjoy a more relaxed sexual relationship with my wife' (p 145)
2 enjoy a better relationship with my children' (p 157)
3 get on better with my marriage partner' (p 167)

Life area C – social and interpersonal relationships

'I would like to be able to . . .
1 control my weight' (p 178)
2 make new friends easily and confidently' (p 194)
3 make a formal or informal speech fluently' (p 204)

Life area D – leisure and sport

'I would like to be able to . . .
1 fly on holiday or on business in a relaxed manner' (p 214)
2 play a game of golf while controlling the effects of stress on key strokes' (p 222)
3 pass my driving test' (p 233)

Even if your own personal goals are not covered in the above twelve, you should find that studying them will provide valuable information which you should be able to make relevant to your own particular ambitions.

How to use the crisis tactics

Because we anticipate that some readers may need to adjust their behaviour very quickly in response to some immediate challenge we have divided each section into two parts. The first of these will be crisis tactics which will be invaluable if only a short amount of time is available for change – for instance with a week to go before an examination, a few days before an interview, a few hours before an important meeting or aircraft journey.

Crisis tactics should be regarded as a type of psychological life-belt to help you stay afloat during an emergency. However, like all life-belts they are designed to provide support not a means of travelling. Once the emergency has passed we recommend that you proceed to develop an effective programme of long-term behaviour modification, and we include detailed explanations of the necessary procedure. You should note, however, that in most cases the crisis tactics can be used in the long-term behaviour modification programme.

Life area A – work and study

In this life area we will deal with difficulties and strategies involved in the following commonly expressed goals:
'I would like to be able to . . .

1 achieve better examination results'
2 create the best impression during interviews'
3 gain faster promotion at work'

Goal one – 'I would like to be able to achieve better examination results.'

Taking an examination means performing a piece of behaviour which is quite separate from the actual subject involved. There are certain principles and skills basic to all types of examination but, unfortunately, these are seldom taught. The assumption seems to be that, provided you have acquired sufficient knowledge of your subject, you will automatically do well in the examination.

This assumption is invalid since high marks in an examination depend as much on an ability to express the available information as on that fund of knowledge being present in the first place.

Once the actual studying has been done and sufficient knowledge exists to answer a satisfactory number of questions, there are two major components to passing an examination:

1 physical skills.
2 mental strategies.

(If your problem is how to acquire the necessary knowledge to take exams then we suggest you read the third section of this life area.)

1 Identifying areas of difficulty

To help you identify the physical skills and mental strategies which may be lacking from your examination-taking behaviour, complete the following ten statements by selecting one or both of the alternatives given which most closely reflect your own behaviour in a similar situation:

1 During the few days before an examination
(a) I have difficulty in sleeping because I become tense and anxious at night. (b) I cannot seem to direct my thoughts coherently towards my studying.

2 On the morning of an examination
(a) I am unable to eat breakfast because my stomach is turning over and I feel I would be sick if food passed my lips. (b) I find ideas are jumbled in my head and I cannot think clearly.

3 Standing outside the examination room just before entering
(a) I sweat, feel sick, experience a high heart rate and tension.
(b) I avoid talking to other people as they seem to be able to remember their facts while all mine have disappeared.

4 When I sit down at the examination desk
(a) The room starts to swim before my eyes, my body reacts with tension and I feel it is going out of control. (b) I keep wondering how I will remember any facts and if I do how will I make sense of them.

5 When I first look at the examination paper
(a) I cannot focus clearly and I keep feeling rising panic as my stomach lurches and my body sweats. (b) I cannot understand the questions and frantically search for one which I can even attempt.

6 Half way through the paper
(a) I feel completely exhausted as though all my energy has been burned up. (b) I realise that there is an easy question which I should have done in place of the one I have completed.

7 When I have selected a question which I think I can do
(a) I find I cannot write quickly enough as my hand develops cramp and discomfort. (b) I can only think of one idea while I know I have studied several others.

8 When I have thought of a few facts for a question
(a) I find I cannot start writing because I am distracted by any small sound or movement which makes me jump. (b) I am unable to write the first sentence and keep writing and re-writing it as time slips away.

9 As the time slips by
(a) I get hotter and hotter as I race to finish the question. (b) I find myself running over time with the early questions and leaving nothing for the final one.

10 At some point during the examination
(a) I have to run from the room in a panic and am completely unable to return. (b) I seem to finish well before time and am unable to go back and fill in any more on the answers I have already written.

If you have scored predominantly a's then a major problem in taking examinations may clearly be physical tension and anxiety. In this case your behaviour modification programme should include learning relaxation skills so that you can reduce stress to a manageable level. For further details see under the Physical Skills heading.

If you have scored predominantly b's then it looks as if a lack of the necessary mental strategies is resulting in difficulties. In this case you should practise the skills listed below under the Mental Strategies heading.

A high score in both areas indicates that a combination of mental and physical barriers is arising to prevent you from taking exams effectively. To remove these barriers you should construct a programme which includes training in both mental and physical skills.

2 Skills and strategies

As we have said, the ability to take examinations effectively must be regarded as a skill in its own right. Many examinees sit down in front of the question papers without practising for the examination in any way and, not surprisingly, they run into trouble.

Physical skills

At a physical level there are two very important skills to be learned before entering the examination room. First of all the muscles which are going to be used must have been trained so that they can cope with extended periods of work without undue exhaustion and cramp. Secondly you must be able to control your anxiety over the situation and keep it to a manageable level.

(*i*) *Muscle training:* Any group of muscles which is made to work unusually hard without prior training will rapidly get tired and may become so tense that it will no longer function properly. The muscles involved in examination-taking, especially those of the neck, back and hands, should be trained by carrying out several extended periods of writing before the actual examination. The most appropriate way of getting this training, of course, is to answer questions, taken from past papers, in mock examinations.

(*ii*) *Anxiety management:* Any examination creates stress and produces anxiety. In small and controlled amounts this is a beneficial response because, as we explained earlier, a slight feeling of tension, a modest amount of adrenalin circulating in the bloodstream, helps to key up the system and enables you to give your best performance. It is when the anxiety becomes acute and handicapping that steps must be taken to reduce the level of stress without completely eliminating the arousal. The secret lies in anxiety management. That is, using the potentially inappropriate response of anxiety as a beneficial and appropriate response which will lead towards goal fulfilment. You can learn anxiety management by perfecting the three types of relaxation which were detailed in the Fourteen-Day Programme.

1 Deep relaxation enables you to identify small increases in stress which could, previously, have passed unnoticed.

2 Quick relaxation is invaluable for settling the autonomic nervous system just prior to starting an examination or to control stress while waiting outside the examination room.

3 Differential relaxation is helpful because it enables you to relax those muscle groups not actually being used and ease tension in those groups being worked unusually hard. This prevents cramp in the hand, arm and shoulders.

When you become experienced at relaxation, and this can be achieved in as little as seven days provided you practise regularly and for a reasonable amount of time each day, your body will learn to react to muscle tension by using it as a signal to relax. In this way tension will be controlled as it occurs.

Mental strategies
The ability to use strategies which help guide mental processes along the most effective route to the desired goal is another valuable ingredient in stress reduction. In the examination situation you will find the following mental strategies extremely useful.

(*i*) *Time allocation:* To use the available time effectively you must devote the first ten or fifteen minutes to reading the questions and writing down a time-table for answering them. Once this time-table has been worked out, stick to it. Use it as a guide to how much time you can devote to each answer and when you must move to the next question. A frequent error amongst students is to spend too long on questions they can answer easily and fully. This sounds like common sense but, in fact, it can be damaging to one's chances of success. This is because the majority of examination questions operate on a principle of diminishing mark returns. While it is fairly easy to pick up the first fifty per cent on each question in the time allowed, it becomes progressively more difficult to earn extra marks. By spending a great deal of time and effort on one question, at the expense of others, you may be able

116

to improve your marks for that particular answer, but it will become increasingly difficult to attain one hundred per cent. This can lead to a failing mark on the paper as a whole. For example, suppose that there are three questions to be answered and you only answer two but do those very well. Instead of picking up, perhaps, 3×55 per cent for the paper, you are awarded 2×70 per cent $+ 1 \times 0$ per cent. This is an average of only forty-seven per cent for the paper as a whole.

Answer all the questions demanded by the examiners.

When you write out your time-table, allocate five or ten minutes for carefully reading through the questions at the start of the paper and leave ten to fifteen minutes for checking your answers at the end.

Save time when answering questions by cross-references between answers rather than by repeating the same information twice.

Never leave the examination room until everyone is told to stop writing. Concentrate on finding new ideas to add to your answers.

(*ii*) *Ideograms:* Before attempting a question write down a list of all the ideas which you can think of relating to the topic. Let them pour out of your memory in any order, to create an ideogram. When you have drained your mind of ideas, use arrows to link them into a logical sequence. As your ideogram fills up, the answer to the question should become increasingly obvious. A sound strategy is to write this ideogram on a clean piece of paper so it can be handed in with the answers, having first neatly crossed it out. By doing this you will allow the examiner to follow your line of thinking on the subject. If, by some accident or because time ran out, you have not been able to include all the key ideas in your actual answer you may still get credit for having thought of them in the first place.

(*iii*) *Revision:* Prepare a list of important facts and figures on a small sheet of paper. Keep this skeleton of ideas as brief as possible but include, if you find them helpful, short sentences or mnemonics which will trigger off a chain of thoughts in your mind. This paper can be studied while waiting to go into the hall. It has the added advantage of concentrating your mind on the subject rather than letting it produce anxiety-increasing thoughts such as how much more knowledge all the other candidates seem to possess! Before you go into the room discard this revision sheet, to avoid the charge of cheating, but reconstruct it as soon as you sit down in the examination room. Before you even bother to read the paper, jot down all the facts and figures which will still be fresh in your memory. You will find that having such a list in front of you increases your confidence.

3 Crisis tactics

If you respond inappropriately to examination situations the only long-term answer is to eliminate such responses using a programme of behaviour modification. But if there is insufficient time to initiate such long-term change at this moment because an examination is due within the next few days, the best thing to do is put into practice the crisis tactics outlined below. These behaviour adjustments can be learned in a couple of days. When the crisis is past, however, you should follow a programme of behaviour change which may include these skills and strategies.

Physical skills
Practise the techniques of relaxation. If time is very short carry out deep relaxation several times a day and use quick relaxation whenever you feel tense during the studying period. Use relaxation before going to sleep and remember that sexual release is a major reducer of tension, and a sleep inducer, especially after an intensive period of study. Do not feel inhibited about this as it can be extremely beneficial.

Mental strategies
If there is no chance to practise setting out a time-table during mock examinations, draw one up before taking the examination using old papers as a guide to what is required, and memorise it. For example, suppose you have a 2.00 p.m. start for a three-hour paper in which three questions have to be answered, the time-table might read like this: 2.00 p.m.–2.15 p.m., reading questions, selecting them, writing out time-table. 2.15 p.m. begin question one. 3.05 p.m. begin question two. 3.55 p.m. begin question three. 4.45

p.m. use the final fifteen minutes for checking what has been written and making any necessary corrections.

The best strategy when answering questions is to start with the one you find easiest as this will give you greater confidence in your overall ability to take the paper. Never answer your best question last because you may run out of time. But, as we have stressed above, never devote time to questions you find easiest at the expense of the others. Stick to the time-table. Do the most difficult question last because, even if you do not have time to complete it, you should have picked up the bulk of the marks on the first two.

Never leave an examination room before the end. If you do feel too tense to carry on and have to walk out, use quick relaxation outside the hall to help you control the tension. Then return to the hall. Avoidance behaviour only makes it harder to remain in the examination hall on the next occasion. By removing yourself from a situation you find stressful you are rewarding yourself with a negative reinforcer. As this reinforcer immediately follows the behaviour it is, as you will understand from reading Part One, extremely powerful in establishing the behaviour. Constant avoidance can lead to the development of a phobia about examinations, by no means an unusual type of phobia.

4 Long-term behaviour modification

Start by going through the Fourteen-Day Programme outlined in Part Two of this book, then carry out the Eight-Day Self-Analysis Programme described in Part Three. Use mock or internal examinations, or any type of paced work, to obtain baseline data. If you are working on your own, create your own examination situations. Use old papers to enable you to identify areas of difficulty and to make the situation as realistic as possible.

Record keeping
As with any other behaviour analysis programme you will record baseline data under the headings of:

Stimulus – the environment in which the behaviour takes place.

Response – what you did.

Example one – Typical entry on day one of monitoring

Life area: A – Work and study

Goal: 'I would like to be able to achieve better examination results'

Behaviour to be monitored: Responses before and during a mock examination

Stimulus	Response	Consequence	'What I would like to have done'
10.05 a.m. In examination hall. Seated at desk. Approx 100 other people present. Mock examination paper in front of me on desk. Blank answer book on desk beside me. Feeling tired through lack of sleep and worn out from anxiety before entering room.	Sat and stared at the exam paper and kept thinking that I could not understand questions. Kept looking at blank answer book and feeling that I would never be able to write even the first sentence. Felt panic begin to rise and my mind becoming more and more devoid of productive thoughts. This lasted for 35 mins.	Felt depressed and even more sure that I would fail the examination because of wasted time. Decided to leave after I had written a few lines.	Sat down immediately and begun to select those questions on which I would have obtained maximum marks. Made an effective time-table to allocate time between answers. Begun writing out rough ideas for my first answer. Would then have felt that I had at least got started and been more inclined to continue.

Consequence – How you or others reacted to what you did.

'*What I would like to have done*' – your desired behaviour under those circumstances.

See Example One.

Structuring a pathway of sub-goals

The analysis will enable you to pin-point those mental and/or physical barriers which are preventing your success in examinations. List these inappropriate pieces of behaviour clearly as in Example One:

1 Inability to relax.

2 Inability to focus attention on understanding each individual question.

3 Inability to write down notes to guide the development of the answers.

The sub-goals towards the overall goal of taking the examination successfully might be arranged as follows:

1 Deep relaxation training.

2 Quick relaxation training.

3 Differential relaxation training.

4 Practising the writing down of ideograms.

5 Reading old exam papers with the object of *really* understanding the questions.

6 Writing an essay at speed while at the same time implementing differential relaxation.

7 Using a previously unseen question to practise comprehension and differential relaxation.

8 Taking an old examination paper, reading through it and extracting your best questions while using differential relaxation.

9 Drawing up ideograms under practice examination conditions.

10 Carrying out full practice examinations using ideograms, directing attention towards comprehension and differential relaxation.

11 Carrying out actual examination making use of the sub-goals previously learned.

Practise these sub-goals using self-reinforcement to establish the pieces of behaviour as you learned during the Fourteen-Day Programme. Suitable reinforcers might be as follows:

Sub-goal	Reinforcers
Relaxation	Reading a book or favourite magazine, listening to music, watching TV programme, having a cup of coffee, smoking a cigarette, having sex.
Practice with creating ideograms	A cigarette, walk, phone a friend, award yourself points towards some major reinforcer: e.g. theatre or cinema outing.
Full examination practice	Buy magazine or small gift. Watch TV programme. Smoke cigarette. Award yourself points towards some major reinforcer.

Remember that it is essential to follow the piece of behaviour immediately with the reinforcer.

Summary

Taking an examination effectively is a piece of behaviour additional to the work of studying and revision which preceded it.

To obtain good marks you have to be able to carry out specific skills successfully. These must be practised during mock examinations.

Physical barriers can be overcome by anxiety management based on relaxation.

Mental barriers can be conquered by learning strategies.

Goal two – 'I would like to be able to create the best impression during interviews'

The ability to make a good impression when being interviewed is a crucial piece of behaviour because an interview is the potential starting point for an important change in one's academic, professional or business lifestyle. We tend, perhaps, to think of interviews as formal affairs before boards or groups of senior executives. But the techniques and strategies which will ensure that you create the best possible impression in such structured interviews will also enable you to put forward your views effectively and confidently under less formal conditions, for example when making a point to a client, discussing a new project with a superior or giving instructions to a subordinate. Each of these situations requires the ability to carry out a specific piece of behaviour which is separate from the content or nature of the interview involved.

1 Identifying areas of difficulty

In order that you can more easily identify barriers which may be restricting your performance at interviews, you should reply to the following ten propositions by selecting one or both of the alternatives given which most closely reflect your own behaviour in a similar situation:

1 When making a request to my superiors
(a) I blush, stammer or become tense in their presence.
(b) I find it difficult to find the right words to present my case.

2 When waiting to be interviewed for a new position
(a) I become tense and anxiously pace the room.
(b) I keep thinking that I will not make a good impression by forgetting to talk about my better qualities.

3 When being interviewed for a new position
(a) I sit awkwardly perched on the edge of my seat.
(b) I find I do not hear some of the questions put to me because I am thinking about what I have to say next.

4 When I am asked to give an account of my previous experience and qualifications
(a) My mouth goes dry and I begin to blush.
(b) I go on rather incoherently about minor incidents in my life.

5 If I am asked an unexpected question and get caught out

(a) I begin to feel very anxious and humiliated.

(b) I try to make up an answer and risk looking foolish.

6 If I am summoned for an unexpected interview with a superior

(a) My heart pounds and I feel sick with anticipation.

(b) I am unable to concentrate on my work because of worry over the interview.

7 When being interviewed

(a) I experience discomfort and inability to breathe in a relaxed fashion. (b) I have difficulty in recalling information about my background.

8 When being interviewed before an audience

(a) I feel my head swimming and my stomach churning with anxiety. (b) I am constantly wondering what the audience is thinking about me.

9 When being interviewed at work

(a) I find I am unable to look the other person in the eyes.

(b) I keep wondering whether he can tell anything detrimental about me from the way I am answering.

10 During the interviews in which my views conflict with others

(a) I find myself stammering incoherently or unable to speak.

(b) I change my arguments so as to agree with the other people.

If you have scored predominantly a's then a major problem in interview situations may well be physical tension and anxiety. In this case your behaviour modification programme should include learning relaxation skills so that you can reduce stress to a manageable level. See details under Physical Skills heading.

If you have scored predominantly b's then it looks as if a lack of the necessary mental strategies is resulting in difficulties. In this case you should practise the skills listed below under the Mental Strategies heading.

A high score in both areas indicates that a combination of mental and physical barriers is arising to prevent you from achieving your full potential at interviews. To remove these barriers you should construct a programme which includes training in both mental and physical skills.

2 Skills and strategies

In Part One we explained that any piece of behaviour which is practised becomes not only more effective but easier to perform. Where formal interviews or the presentation of views in an informal setting are concerned the same rule applies. Informal meetings may be frequent occurrences and, therefore, pieces of behaviour which you can practise in reality. Where formal, job or university entrance type interviews are concerned such practice may be neither possible nor advisable. You *could* apply for positions merely for the sake of gaining experience in being interviewed, but this would involve a considerable expenditure of time. It is far more likely that when you apply for a position you will really want to obtain it and will, therefore, need to create the best impression at the interview.

For this reason several of the skills under both the physical and the mental headings will need to be practised in artificial or mock surroundings with, perhaps, some friends or relatives playing the role of the interviewers. But do not despise such rehearsals because of any sense of unreality you feel. They are valuable learning sessions which will help you iron out your strategies and approaches to effective presentation of your best qualities.

Physical skills

(*i*) *Tension and anxiety:* Learn the procedures of relaxation detailed in the Fourteen-Day Programme and concentrate especially on learning to relax quickly so that you can use the skill should you be called upon to take an unexpected interview or in the event of something especially stressful arising during the course of an interview. Differential relaxation is also valuable as it will enable you to sit comfortably without muscle tension while talking.

(*ii*) *Speaking:* Use a tape-recorder to rehearse answers to the most likely questions. Practise answering such questions in a relaxed and confident manner, keeping your voice level adjusted to the size of the room in which you are speaking. Nothing is more irritating for members of a large interview board, who often sit in large board rooms, than a candidate who mumbles. Remember too that some members of interview boards may be elderly and slightly deaf! Learn to speak clearly as well as with sufficient volume. A common mistake with inexperienced speakers is that they tend to talk *too fast*. With the tape recorder practise delivering your words at the rate of about one hundred per minute. This is the speed which professional broadcasters generally use. It is rapid enough to sustain interest yet not so fast that words and ideas will get lost along the way.

Breathing correctly is of great importance and one of the chief difficulties of physical tension is that it makes respiration fast and uneven. Practise taking a breath and speaking, without inhaling again. Use your stomach and diaphragm muscles to expel the air at an even rate. Try and pace your answers so that you never get caught short of breath. Use pauses not merely to emphasise some point in your reply but also to take a breath. When you play back your tape-recorded answers listen carefully to your inflexion and volume at the end of each sentence. There is a common tendency to let the voice go down, to fade out the last few words so that they are barely audible. Try to end instead by emphasising your final words so as to underline your points verbally.

(iii) Body movement: Practise walking into a room with a firm and confident step. People inexperienced in performing before an audience, even the small audience formed by an interview board, tend to be very self-conscious about their hands. You can thrust them into your pockets, but this may give a slovenly impression. A better alternative is to link them loosely behind your back if you have to stand or to fold them in your lap or over one knee when seated. Try not to fiddle around with them as this can be irritating and distracting for your audience. The interviewer may say that you can smoke if you wish. Before doing so make quite certain that there is an ash tray conveniently close to hand. Some interviewers like to stress their subjects by inviting them to smoke when there is nowhere, except the carpet, for them to drop their ash. With this and similar tactics you should plan ahead so as not to be taken off guard. For instance, sudden unexpected questions by a previously silent and apparently disinterested board member should be considered for a few seconds and then replied to evenly and in a relaxed tone.

(iv) Eye-contact: Many people find it hard to maintain eye-

126

contact with the person to whom they are speaking. If this is your problem, use your training sessions to practise this skill. Eye-contact establishes a vital non-verbal link between two people, and imparts a sense of honesty and confidence. If you look down at the floor or up at the ceiling when answering, your reply is likely to make less of a personal impression on the person who asked the question. There is no need to maintain eye-contact throughout your reply and a fixed gaze could be embarrassing. But maintain eye-contact especially while starting and finishing your answer.

Mental strategies

(*i*) *Pre-planning:* Preparation for any interview or meeting is essential. If you are applying for a job or seeking a place at a college or university it will pay you to have researched the background of the company or organisation you are hoping to join. If you are going into an interview to negotiate, put forward a new proposal or defend a policy you must have an overall grasp of the concept involved. In the first case such knowledge, judiciously inserted into your answers, will help produce a good overall impression. In the second case it will prevent your being thrown by some unexpected and, perhaps quite invalid, counter-argument. If, during either situation, a point is raised to which you do not know the answer then be prepared to say so. Do not pretend to a knowledge which you do not possess or you may get caught out. In that case you will look more foolish than if you had admitted your ignorance – in a positive way – in the first place. You might accomplish this by saying, for example: 'I am afraid I don't have that particular statistic at my disposal right now, but I can easily check it for you.' If your background planning has been adequate, however, it should be impossible to catch you out on any obvious or major point.

When you have done your research, write down the key points on a small piece of card and carry it with you to the interview. While waiting, read through the notes. This, together with quick relaxation, will help you to prevent becoming tense during the last few minutes as well as refreshing your memory.

(*ii*) *Answering questions:* Concentrate on the positive aspects of your career or arguments while playing down any more negative points. Remember that you are your own public relations officer and you must do a good selling job on yourself – after all, nobody else there will! Pause for a few seconds before answering a question, even if the answer is right on your lips. A swift reply may be taken for an ill-considered one. Remember that speaking without thinking is like shooting without aiming.

Use positive reinforcement procedures when answering rather than trying to score points and making a foolish questioner feel, and perhaps look, stupid. In the long run such punishing responses on your part are more likely to harm you rather than him. Positive reinforcement involves selecting any sensible features of an otherwise ill-considered question and playing them up. Saying, for example: 'Well that's a very interesting question . . .' or 'I think that's a very interesting way of looking at the situation . . .'

In a negotiating situation apply the same technique and build on any positive contributions whilst ignoring or playing down the more negative aspects of the proposals. Exchanges which feature the 'If you don't do this I won't do that . . .' are all too common in confrontations and are totally negative. They usually lead to deadlock or at best, ill-feeling. Approach all situations with an 'If you *will* do this I *will* do that . . .' attitude and positive progress can usually be made.

Never push your opponent into a corner. Always allow an avenue of dignified retreat. Look on all interviews and discussions as a game of chess. The object, as in chess, is to win the game, not take your opposite number's pieces for the sake of it. Remember, incidentally, that these rules may be as important in marital situations as in the board room (see Life Area B, Section Three).

(*iii*) *Appearance:* In order to feel confident and positive about yourself you must dress in a way which is comfortable and appropriate to the environment. Do not buy new clothes and only put them on a few hours before the interview. They will be stiff and, perhaps, slightly uncomfortable. Feel easy about your clothes and personal appearance so that you can concentrate all your efforts on answering the questions.

3 Crisis tactics

If an interview is imminent and you have encountered mental or physical barriers in the past, there may not be time to carry out a full behaviour modification programme. Under these circumstances use the following guidelines, but note that these tactics can be used as a long-term behaviour modification programme.

1 Spend as much time as possible practising relaxation. Carry out several sessions of deep relaxation during the days prior to the interview, and use quick relaxation at odd moments. Use quick relaxation when waiting just before being called in for an interview.

2 With a friend or relative spend a little time practising answers to the most likely questions. In a job interview you are most certainly going to have to talk about your qualifications, educational and social background, hobbies and extra-mural activities. Be prepared for the frequently posed final question: 'Now is there anything you would like to ask us?' Such a question is usually far more than a polite formality on the part of the interviewers. They often consider that it provides important insights into the interviewee's motives and attitudes. Try to ask a question about the organisation rather than one which relates to you personally. If you have had time to do some background research this should help you to make your question more interesting and significant.

3 Practise retaining eye-contact for a large part of the time when replying to a question.

4 Practise keeping your breathing regular and relaxed.

4 Long-term behaviour modification

First of all follow the Fourteen-Day Programme in Part Two and when you have familiarised yourself with the principles and skills described begin a Seven-Day Analysis Programme based on your particular interview situations.

Record keeping

As in the Seven-Day Analysis Programme you will be recording baseline data about your interview behaviour under four main headings.

Stimulus – the environment in which the behaviour takes place.
Response – what you did.
Consequence – how you or others reacted to what you did.
'*What I would like to have done*' – your desired behaviour under those circumstances.

See Example Two.

Structuring a pathway of sub-goals

In Example Two the following pieces of inappropriate behaviour can be identified:

1 Inability to relax and to control anxiety during interviews.
2 Inability to present ideas effectively.
3 Inability to recall important facts under stress.
4 Lack of confidence needed to be assertive when the situation demands it.

The major sub-goals in a programme of behaviour modification for dealing with clients and subordinates might be:

1 Quick and differential relaxation training.

2 Preparation of logical and significant points in any argument or discussion.

3 Adequate record keeping so that details of each client's needs are available.

4 Learning to respond assertively in appropriate situations. This will involve practising behaviour consistent with the feelings of anger or firmness without actually losing your temper. This may be accomplished by practising such confrontations with a relative or friend before it occurs. This behaviour includes steady eye-contact, good voice projection and enunciation, a sitting posture which varies between relaxed with back against the back of chair and firm with the body leaning slightly towards the other person. Expressive arm movements will underline comments.

Example two – Typical entry on day one of monitoring

Life area: A – Work and study

Goal: 'I would like to be able to create the best impression during interviews'

Behaviour to be monitored: Reponses before and during interviews

Stimulus	Response	Consequence	'What I would like to have done'
2.30 p.m. Waiting room outside interview room. Five other candidates present. No-one talking. Feeling upset and gnawing pain in stomach. Probably due to not having eaten anything during the day because of feeling of sickness prior to the interview. Thinking of bad impression made at last interview and how important this is for my future and the security of my family.	Sat trying to gather my thoughts about what to say. Could only think of my failings and knew that I would probably emphasise my poor university degree as on previous occasions rather than my extensive practical knowledge of the areas.	Noticed other candidates watching me. Sure they could see me sweating and becoming red. Had to sit on my hands to stop them shaking. When entered interview room found my mind a blank and my speech hesitant and stammering in answering questions.	Sat in waiting room and gone over my good qualities, perhaps jotting down some notes on paper to refresh my thoughts. Been able to eat to remove the pains in my stomach. Been able to appear at ease and look as confident as others did. Not trembled. When being interviewed remained calm and in control of the situation. Used my planned answers flexibly in the interview.

5 A readiness to acknowledge one of the offender's good points while pointing out his failures.

6 Guiding subordinates by giving appropriate instructions. Punishment and criticism are far less effective than positive reinforcement.

These sub-skills should be learned using positive reinforcement methods so that each time a piece of desired behaviour is carried out it can be followed immediately by a reward. You can use the list system of minor and major reinforcers selecting those which are most suitable and practical for the behaviour which you are learning. Where it is not possible to use an immediate reward, then the points system can be successfully utilised. Award yourself marks and use these to buy some major reward. As you become more proficient in the new skills you will also be reinforced by the more successful ways in which you are able to function in your working environment and the increasing opportunities for promotion (see also Goal Three).

Summary

Creating the best impression at interviews is a piece of skilled behaviour which can be learned.

To present yourself in the best light you have to carry out skills of physical and mental preparation which can be practised in mock situations with friends.

Physical barriers can be overcome by relaxation procedures, while mental barriers may be removed by acquiring strategies for presentation of material.

Goal three – 'I would like to be able to gain faster promotion at work'

Many people in business who have the energy, enthusiasm and experience needed to gain promotion find themselves unable to realise their full career potential because of a lack of structure and discipline in their approach to work. As a result they squander their energy and efforts on ill-directed routes towards their overall goal. Failure to achieve promotion, a realisation that younger and perhaps – in their view at least – less able men are being promoted over their heads leads to frustration, disappointment, a loss of motivation and a decline in confidence. These combine to reduce their effectiveness and make it increasingly less likely that they will achieve the promotion they desire and probably deserve.

A basic building block of success in any working situation, and one which enables you to direct your time and efforts appropriately, is work scheduling. Effective scheduling ensures that all your energies are productively spent, increases the speed and ease with which work loads are accomplished and allows you to achieve more in the same amount of time with no extra exertion. The principles involved are especially useful for career advancement but they can equally well be used in any working situation, for example when studying for an examination or when looking after the household.

1 Identifying areas of difficulty

To help you identify which barriers to your gaining faster promotion are in operation you should answer the following ten questions by selecting one, or both, of the alternatives given which most closely reflect your own behaviour in a similar situation.

1 On sitting down to plan a project for the current day
(a) My mind wanders and I am easily distracted by other thoughts.
(b) I start to fidget or feel tense.

2 On looking at a backlog of work which has piled up
(a) I think how hopeless it all is and do nothing for the rest of the day but add to the backlog. (b) I become panicky and attempt to sort out so much of the backlog that I skip unproductively from topic to topic.

3 When confronted by an unexpected change of direction
(a) I am unable to shift my attention from its usual groove.
(b) I panic at the thought of not being able to cope.

4 When I am required to give staff their instructions for the day or the week

(a) I find that I cannot delegate authority to them. (b) I become tongue-tied and unable to express my wishes.

5 When I open a book or report to study specific passages in order to gain information

(a) I become sleepy and read and re-read the same sections without remembering them. (b) I begin to doodle and fiddle with objects on the desk.

6 At the end of a day's work or study

(a) I feel that I am no further towards understanding the problem. (b) I am physically exhausted and find it difficult to unwind.

7 When under pressure

(a) My attention wanders and my concentration falters even more. (b) I become irritable and tense with others.

8 When faced with a particular task or project

(a) I seek perfection and repeat the same procedures time and again, never feeling satisfied with the results. (b) I am so daunted by the prospects of the task that I break out in a sweat with despair.

9 When faced with a difficult or unpleasant task

(a) I constantly seek out work to occupy me. (b) I rush around trying to divert myself from the job in hand by wasting time chatting, drinking coffee and other similar activities.

10 When faced with a lot of facts and figures from which I am to make sense

(a) I find I am unable to produce concise summaries or sort important information from that which is irrelevant. (b) I make copious notes and wear myself out while realising that much of the information is superfluous.

If you have scored predominantly a's then it looks as if a lack of the necessary mental strategies is producing difficulties. In this case you should practise the skills described below under the Mental Strategies heading.

If you have scored predominantly b's then a major problem in work scheduling is clearly physical tension and anxiety. In this case your behaviour modification programme should include learning relaxation skills so that you can reduce stress to a manageable level. See details under the Physical Skills heading.

A high score in both areas indicates that a combination of mental and physical barriers is arising to prevent you from working effectively. To remove these barriers you should construct a programme which includes training in both mental and physical skills.

2 Skills and strategies

Work scheduling, the planning of an effective working day which will enable you to direct your energies and experience along the most productive lines, is a piece of behaviour separate from the actual work involved.

You may find that you work better at some times of the day than others. We all have different body rhythms which result in our being most efficient during certain periods – early morning or late evening for example. If possible you should structure your schedule to take account of these productive periods. But even if this is not possible and you have to work at times other than those most favourable, you will find that the skills and strategies set out below will help you work more easily and effectively.

Physical skills

(i) *Dealing with stress and anxiety:* The ability to relax deeply, quickly or only in certain of the muscle groups, is an essential skill in combating anxiety and tension. You should learn the procedures of deep, quick and differential relaxation as described in the Fourteen-Day Programme of Part Two.

It is particularly important to have good, restful sleep at night. Relaxation will help you here as will some of the mental strategies described below. People with work problems very often find themselves trapped in a particular vicious negative halo effect. Worry at work makes them stressed and irritable at home. This means that leaving the work environment produces no lessening of tension. Instead of finding relaxation in their free-time they encounter only further negative interactions as their family and friends respond to their own stress-induced impatience and irritation. As a result, their night's sleep is often disturbed and fails adequately to rest the body. The morning finds them as tense and anxious as on the

135

previous evening and so the halo effect progresses. The important thing to remember, as we explained in Part One, is that the chain reaction is only apparently unbreakable. By using relaxation and strategies to sort out mental confusion you can swiftly snap the links.

(*ii*) *Eating correctly:* Diet is another important physical consideration and one which, like sleep, is frequently upset by work problems. A snatched cup of coffee before leaving the house, a sandwich instead of lunch and a large meal at night, eaten with no particular appetite or interest, are all too often the gastronomic lot of the stressed worker.

The cells of the muscles, brain and nervous system burn sugar, supplied by the bloodstream, to produce their energy. The amount of sugar in the blood is, therefore, critical to the way that both body and mind respond. A person who has gone without food for twelve hours will usually have between 80 and 120 milligrams of sugar per 100cc of blood; the average is about 95 milligrams per 100cc. When the sugar level falls to around 70 milligrams per 100cc the person will start to feel hungry and tire quickly. When the blood sugar level drops to 65 milligrams the person may feel distinctly uncomfortable, with a rumbling stomach and a desire to eat sweets. If the level is allowed to drop still further then tiredness may turn into exhaustion. Headaches develop and the body becomes tense. This fall in blood sugar level produces irritation and depression. The low sugar sufferer is typically moody and uncooperative.

Research has shown that the speed with which sugar is released into the bloodstream from digestion depends on the amounts of protein and fat taken in with it. If there is a balance then the sugar is released over a period of hours, making it available to the body much more regularly. Sugar taken in with very little or no protein or fat burns quickly, produces a spurt of energy, and is gone.

Unfortunately Western eating habits make it unlikely that sugar is taken into the body in the most effective way. The average breakfast is high on starch and sugar but very low on protein. As a result the energy is released too early and by mid-morning the blood sugar level starts to fall. An 11 o'clock cup of coffee or tea does very little to ease the situation, and a snatched lunch only compounds the problem. By evening the body is listless and lethargic. Everything seems too much of an effort. At night, it is true, we tend to eat a proper balanced meal. But often the energy which this releases into the bloodstream goes to waste. The general exhaustion produced by the day makes us sleepy and, with a heavy stomach, we may doze before the television until it is time to stumble upstairs to bed. What happens to the excess sugar produced but not used? It remains in the bloodstream. The following morning our blood sugar level is still high. So high that we have no appetite for a sensible high protein breakfast. We drink some coffee, eat a slice of toast and depart for work. The wheel has turned full circle.

Ideally the day should start with a breakfast high in protein, fat and sugar. Lunch should be equally balanced to release energy slowly during the afternoon, while the evening meal should be light so that we sleep without indigestion and wake up with our blood sugar level low enough to have an appetite for breakfast. In practice this may not be possible, although if you can reorganise your eating habits in this way you will notice a rapid and beneficial result. Failing this, try to top up your blood sugar level during the day by a mid-morning snack. Avoid sweets, chocolate, cream cakes if possible as these can be harmful to the teeth and waistline without being especially valuable to the digestion. The ideal mid-morning break is a glass of milk and some fresh fruit.

(*iii*) *Periods of rest:* It is far more effective to take a thirty-minute rest break in a series of six five-minute rest periods than all at once. Try and take a short rest after each period of concentrated activity. During this break leave the working environment, even if you only walk down the corridor, step outside for a quick breath of air or go to buy a newspaper. The fact that you have removed yourself physically from the stimulus of the office or work area will be beneficial. During this break carry out quick relaxation to reduce tension. If you feel that there is simply not enough time to take a long enough lunch break to eat a proper meal, then leave the office to have your sandwiches or snack. As your work scheduling improves, however, you should find that the time becomes available to take a sensible lunch break. Remember that in the same way as a painter has to stand back from a canvas to get an overall view of the picture, so you too, need to distance yourself from your efforts to get your work into perspective.

Mental strategies

(i) *Dealing with backlogs:* As most work programmes are continuing ones, it is impractical to stop and clear up a backlog before returning to the projects in hand. To attempt to do so is, usually, self-defeating as current workload left unattended merely becomes tomorrow's in-tray constipation.

The most effective strategy is, so far as possible, to disregard the backlog and concentrate all your efforts on the new projects. Only when these are well in hand should you turn your attention to outstanding work. You should then work out a timetable which allows you sufficient periods each day to whittle down the backlog whilst keeping up to date with ongoing projects.

(ii) *Establishing a realistic timetable:* By making a total of the number of hours you can realistically spend on your work in any one week you will arrive at a maximum figure to be distributed amongst the different projects. For instance a business man working a forty-hour week might find himself with a total of thirty hours left after deducting the time required for conferences and meetings. These thirty hours have to be distributed amongst planning a new market survey, making a presentation to a client, interviewing applicants for a new post and organising a research team. He would have to assess how much time would be needed for each task and when they would need to be slotted into his working week. Time must be left on the programme to allow spare capacity in which to deal with mistakes, delays and the inevitable set-backs. Practical experience has indicated that filling a timetable to about eighty per cent capacity gives it sufficient flexibility to cope with all but the direst emergencies.

Once you have decided how much time each ongoing project will require the next step is to slot each one into the working week. An important rule should be observed here. Try to carry out the more difficult, distasteful or uncreative tasks in a period immediately before carrying out a pleasurable activity – for example a mid-morning break or the end of the working day when you can look forward to going home and relaxing. Such tactics will help you to establish the more difficult or less pleasant pieces of behaviour by positive reinforcement. They also make it less likely for a negative halo effect to start.

(*iii*) *Involving others:* Depending on your personality you may also find it useful to involve other people in your work problems more than you do at present. Many people find it easier to come to a decision or create a new project after discussing the situation with a friend or colleague. Be careful, however, that discussion does not become an excuse for delaying a project. Some companies and many government departments become completely clogged up by inter-office memos, requests, forms and similar red-tape. Use discussion as a stimulus to activity, not an avoidance technique.

(*iv*) *Briefing colleagues and subordinates:* Before giving instructions to members of the staff or going into a discussion with colleagues, be certain that you are fully briefed on the project and have an overall view of the problems and issues which you want to discuss with them. Provide yourself with an agenda and tick off the main points as they are dealt with. If you allow yourself to be side-tracked into non-essential issues time will be wasted and confusion amongst the others may result.

(*v*) *Coping with inattention:* During a period assigned for work on a particular project in your timetable you may find yourself unable to concentrate. Perhaps your vision starts to blur, you re-read the same passage several times and begin to feel sleepy and bored. If this happens you should not force yourself to concentrate but get up and leave the working environment for a few minutes. From what we have said earlier in the book you will realise that by remaining in an environment whilst feeling sleepy and bored you are likely to come under stimulus control from the surroundings which will, eventually, always trigger off feelings of tiredness and disinterest. To prevent this negative stimulus control from being established, walk away from the working environment, spend a few minutes engaged in some other activity – talking,

139

smoking a cigarette, drinking a cup of coffee – and then return to the task.

(*vi*) *Coping with distractions:* The best way to deal with temptation is to give in to it! But do so in a controlled way. If you find your attention wandering after a period of concentrated effort and you want to doodle or stare out of the window, then allow yourself this relaxation but build these short rest periods into your timetable and make provision for them when scheduling your workload. Such small, pleasurable activities can be looked on as reinforcers helping to establish the piece of behaviour which they follow. Bear them in mind when working out a long-term behaviour modification programme. The advantage of allowing for and planning on brief periods of unwinding is that you can then indulge in them without feeling guilty about wasting time.

(*vii*) *Accepting realistic standards:* For many people the idea that they should teach themselves to make do with less than perfection will come close to heresy. We are not saying here that you should lower your sights to turn out slipshod or inadequate work. But in reality the perfectionist is seldom the most effective member of a workforce. The law of diminishing returns is a useful one to remember here. You may carry out a project for one client which is ninety-five per cent perfect but has taken six times longer than it should have done. In the same time you might have been able to produce six projects which were eighty per cent perfect which resulted in almost identical goodwill and far greater material benefits. The story of the very brilliant professor of literature at an American university illustrates this point. He was always claiming that, given time, he could write the world's most outstanding novel. One day his students, tired of hearing this boast, locked him into his study and said they would only release him after he had completed the first twenty lines of this work. Eight hours later, when they finally released the exhausted and shattered academic, his desk was surrounded by torn up paper but not a single word had been written and kept. Each time he wrote a line, he explained, he realised its inadequacies and short-comings and had to begin again. He sought perfection so he was never satisfied. As a result he never produced anything, good, bad or indifferent. Strive for the best possible work within the timetable you have set yourself.

(*viii*) *Learning to make a start:* Many people find it difficult to know where to begin a complex project. The answer is to start anywhere you like, beginning, middle or even at the end, but make a start. Blank sheets of paper are daunting and confidence deflating. Sheets with writing on them, even if the actual words need a tremendous amount of redrafting and revision, give you something concrete to work with. Set your thoughts, however ill-defined you feel them to be, down on paper rather than sit with them unresolved in your mind.

(*ix*) *Learning to become objective:* If there is time, set your finished work aside and come back to it the following day. Start on another task, anything which will divert your mind from the first project, before returning to revise and complete the first piece of work. In this way you can often assess your efforts more easily and objectively since, on returning to the work, you will look at it from a slightly different perspective.

3 Crisis tactics

If your work has been wearing you down mentally and physically you may be too tired and anxious to attempt a major behaviour modification programme at this point in time. In this case we suggest that you implement the following crisis strategies to give yourself a breathing space. Then, when the situation has started to resolve itself, you can begin to work on long-term change.

Physical barriers
Learn the techniques of relaxation. Use deep relaxation immediately prior to going to sleep so that you get a really restful night. When writing out your timetable, slot in a frequent number of short rest periods. Use quick relaxation during these breaks and before any stressful meetings. Look at your diet and try to modify it so that your blood sugar level remains topped up throughout the working day.

Mental skills
Draw up a timetable and keep this to hand at all times. Make the schedule sufficiently flexible to include the rest periods discussed

above, plus additional time for coping with delays and set-backs. If there is a backlog of work then set aside time on your schedule for coping with this, but do not push aside ongoing projects so as to empty your in-tray. Treat your timetable as a guide, it may have to be abandoned on some days when a completely unexpected piece of work crops up, but when sticking to it, do so quite firmly. Do not let work encroach on your rest periods. Use the system of reinforcing difficult tasks by following them with something pleasurable. Do not wait around for the right mood to begin work. Get started.

4 Long-term behaviour modification

Start by following the Fourteen-Day Programme so as to gain experience with the necessary skills. Now carry out a Seven-Day Self-Analysis Programme aimed at establishing baseline data in the main problem areas. The ten question inventory and the description of mental and physical barriers given earlier should have helped you to identify the particular problems which you are encountering. It is these pieces of inappropriate behaviour which must be closely examined during the analysis period.

Record keeping
As with all analysis charts you will be recording baseline data under four headings:

Stimulus – the environment in which the behaviour takes place.
Response – what you did.
Consequence – how you or others reacted to what you did.
'*What I would like to have done*' – your desired behaviour under those circumstances.

See Example three.

Structuring a pathway of sub-goals
In Example three the following pieces of inappropriate behaviour can be identified:

1 Inability to allocate time effectively.
2 Inability to state requirements accurately.

142

Example three – Typical entry on day one of monitoring

Life area: A – Work and study

Goal: 'I would like to be able to gain faster promotion at work'

Behaviour to be monitored: Work scheduling during a typical week

Stimulus	Response	Consequence	'What I would like to have done'
9.15 a.m. Entering office first thing in morning. Thoughts jumping between several projects in mind. Presented on desk with full in-tray and two reports to be read. Know that have to allocate staff procedures today.	Feel cold sweat and sit at desk completely unable to think which job has priority. Flip through a report but cannot take it in.	Spend 45 minutes with no positive result. In dabbling find anxiety rising as the deadlines for allocations of procedures to staff advance. Staff seem confused about what is expected.	Apply myself solely to one task on arrival at office. Worked against the clock without stress and put myself into a position where I am sufficiently prepared to brief the staff effectively.

3 Inability to extract key points from complex material.

The major sub-goals in a programme of behaviour modification might be:

1 Draw up a schedule of time available and tasks to be completed.
2 Construct a weekly timetable which includes periods of relaxation.
3 Draw up agendas to make staff meetings more productive.
4 Practise the presentation of material from the agenda to staff.
5 Use differential and quick relaxation to reduce stress and enable workload to be dealt with calmly.
6 Learn speed reading to help get through piles of documents swiftly.

You should practise these skills and strategies using the techniques of self-reinforcement explained in the Fourteen-Day Programme. Remember to use any small reward, such as coffees, cigarettes, reading a favourite magazine and so on as well as using a points system whereby you award yourself points immediately after carrying out one of the skills and later cashing them in by allowing yourself a large reinforcement.

Summary

Although the actual capabilities for carrying out work may be present it does not follow this potential will be realised. In cases where work scheduling is difficult it is possible to acquire this skill by learning processes.

Important physical and mental skills to overcome the various barriers which may prevent your potential from being realised, have to be practised.

After using these new methods for several days it will become progressively easier to streamline your working hours so that you not only accomplish more, but do so without stress or anxiety.

Life area B – Family, marriage, sex and intimacy

In this life area we will deal with difficulties and strategies involved in the following commonly expressed goals:
'I would like to be able to . . .

1 enjoy a more relaxed sexual relationship with my wife'
2 enjoy a better relationship with my children'
3 get on better with my marriage partner'

Goal One – 'I would like to be able to enjoy a more relaxed sexual relationship with my wife.'

The ability to respond affectionately and effectively in a sexual situation is, perhaps, one of the most crucial pieces of behaviour in our repertoire. It is also amongst the least practised and most taboo shrouded activities in our culture. As a result what should be a source of mutual pleasure and giving often becomes furtive, embarrassing and guilt-ridden, affording little enjoyment or satisfaction to either party. Over the past decade we have become increasingly *preoccupied* with sex yet no more *occupied* with it and, as a result, fantasised and absurd values have been attached to it.

Many of the problems can be attributed to misinformation generated by the popular media and the exploitation of sex by the advertising industry. Even sex therapy has become a cultish and fashionable area by which to profit from sexual anxieties. Fashionable chains of sex therapy clinics now abound in many parts of the Western world and it is noteworthy that there exists a close correlation between the level of cultural attainment in a society and the number and types of professional intervention in sexual matters which it generates.

Schools of thought exist which hold that sexual behaviour is an inbuilt function which needs no learning – and in theory this is correct. In the primitive state animals and humans will engage in uninhibited and, consequently, stress-free, sexual acts. In modern society such a state of innocence is impossible. We have learned to become over-conscious about our sexual activities and to try to fit our personal sexual expression into cultural constraints, from religious taboos to exaggerated concepts of sexual athleticism.

This frequently results in our trying to perform a natural function in an unnatural way and so leading ourselves to stress and anxiety. The negative halo effects generated by tense and strained sexual relationships are considerable and damaging. Tension at home can lead to an overall sense of frustration, a lowering of confidence in general and, frequently, a need to escape from reality in drink or extra-marital sex which in turn only increases the problems.

1 Identifying areas of difficulty

In order to clarify the areas of stress and tension in your sex life you should complete the following ten statements by selecting one, or both, of the alternatives given which most closely reflect your own behaviour in a similar situation:

1 When making love to my spouse
(a) I find my body becoming tense with anxiety. (b) I wonder whether I am doing things normally.

2 In an intimate situation where sex might be a possibility
(a) I become embarrassed and may have to leave my partner.
(b) I am unable to express my feelings verbally to my partner.

3 When in a sexual situation with my partner
(a) I have difficulty achieving erection/becoming lubricated and aroused. (b) I experience difficulty in telling my partner how I feel.

4 When having sexual intercourse with my partner
(a) I struggle to keep control/bring about my orgasm. (b) My mind wanders on to subjects other than the present sexual situation.

5 If I experience any discomfort or dissatisfaction during sex
(a) I simply tense up and continue to put up with it. (b) I am unable to communicate my needs to my partner.

6 When I am being approached and caressed in the early stages of lovemaking

(a) My body tenses and I begin to feel uneasy. (b) I find myself wondering whether this attempt at sex will be a failure.

7 After having had sex
(a) I feel unsatisfied and still physically tense. (b) I feel I did not understand my partner's needs and my partner did not understand mine.

8 When I masturbate
(a) I feel uncomfortable and rush to get it completed. (b) I feel ashamed that I had to resort to it.

9 During foreplay and coitus with my partner
(a) I have difficulty in touching my own body and demonstrating how I like to be stimulated. (b) I feel inhibited about showing directly or explaining what arouses me.

10 In conversation with my partner
(a) I become physically tongue-tied and have to change the subject if sex is mentioned. (b) I feel guilty and ashamed to discuss sex.

If you have scored predominantly a's then a major problem in achieving a successful sex life is likely to be physical tension. In this case your behaviour modification programme should include learning relaxation skills so that you can reduce anxiety to a manageable level. See details under the Physical Skills heading.

If you have scored predominantly b's then it looks as if a lack of the necessary mental strategies is resulting in difficulties. In this case you should practise the skills listed below under the Mental Strategies heading.

A high score in both areas suggests that a combination of mental and physical barriers is arising to prevent you from having successful sexual intercourse. To remove these barriers you should construct a programme which includes training in both mental and physical skills.

2 Skills and strategies

At first it may seem unusual to think of sexual activity as a piece of skilled behaviour, but if we adopt this starting point it allows us to develop ways in which difficult sexual barriers can be removed. Sexual activity comprises both mental strategies and physical skills. Mental strategies include knowledge of the anatomy and physiology of both sexes, attitudes which allow uninhibited expression of emotion and the ability to communicate needs and wishes to a partner in a sexual relationship. Physical skills include the ability to relax and to allow natural responses such as erection and lubrication to occur. Consideration of all these skills in turn will enable you to put together a programme for sexual fulfilment tailored specifically to your own needs.

Physical skills

(*i*) *Relaxation training:* Since deep and quick relaxation are *parasympathetic* responses, as is sexual arousal, it follows that relaxation methods can be used to remove physical barriers to sexual enjoyment. The usual problem in physical sexual barriers is tension and anxiety brought about by the fear of failure, when the response should be one of accepting a caress or sexual advance in a relaxed state. If you can attain a level of deep relaxation – and a good way to do this is for you and your partner to learn to relax together, preferably in a comfortable room where you will be uninterrupted – future moves towards sexual arousal will stand much more chance of succeeding than if you enter the sexual arena tense and nervous. Use the techniques described in the Fourteen-Day Programme to guide you.

(*ii*) *Explore your physical responses:* Two skills are useful in discovering how your own and your partner's bodies respond.

The first is by using masturbation while away from your partner. Clinical and research evidence suggests that for both men and women masturbation carried out in an unashamed way can be of benefit to future sexual relationships with a partner. For instance, research has shown that women who have masturbated to orgasm are three times as likely to enjoy orgasm with male partners than women who have not. Also, men who have enjoyed relaxed and uninhibited masturbation are much less likely to lose control of ejaculation than those who have masturbated quickly and furtively and taught themselves to ejaculate rapidly. So do not be ashamed to explore your own bodily responses through masturbation. You will later be in a position to discuss and demonstrate with your partner the methods of stimulation which you like best.

Secondly it is important, especially if there is a sexual problem, to set aside a period of time each day (this may be just a few minutes or much longer according to your personal timetable and tastes) when you simply explore, caress, massage, and guide one another to discover how to give and receive pleasure from your partner. Try to programme this into every day as it is all too easy to find excuses not to bother. Very rarely, however, is it completely impossible to spend just a few minutes in mutual physical caressing and you should be careful not to convince yourself that your life is 'too hectic for that sort of thing'.

(*iii*) *Explore your partner's responses:* It is important to remember that, for most people, sexually sensitive zones may not be limited to small areas but can be found almost everywhere on the body. In discovering your partner's erogenous zones you should learn how to give a massage all over while being gentle but firm and accepting feedback about the way in which you are moving your hands. Use an oil or a powder so that irritation of the skin is avoided and spend some time regularly exploring each other's bodies in this way. Remember also that both sexes produce smells and tastes in their genital areas which are designed to be sexually arousing to their partners. So do not be shy of including oral stimulation, so long as this does not present anxiety. If it does, you can progress slowly to this stage, if you have any desire to reach it, using relaxation as a means of overcoming any embarrassment or anxiety.

Such activities, which do not include insertion of the penis into the vagina, should not simply be considered as passing phases of less importance than the final goal of intercourse, but as pleasurable and sexually rewarding goals in themselves. In fact, it is those couples who occasionally pet, caress and generally have fun in an intimate setting, while not feeling they have to go on to coitus, who most frequently report their sex life is very satisfying.

Professional experience has indicated that even couples who are sexually experienced may lack some of the basic and more detailed information about the physiology involved. While they are not essential to the enjoyment of sex, such fundamental facts can be useful building blocks in constructing a more varied sexual repertoire.

Let us look first at the male who is stimulating his female partner, either manually or orally. An important location of very heightened sensual pleasure in the female is the clitoris which can be found most easily when the woman lies on her back with her knees drawn up slightly and her legs spread apart. If the lips covering the vagina are parted and a finger drawn gently from the vaginal opening up towards the navel, the small, hard protuberance of the clitoris will be felt between half an inch to an inch away from the vaginal opening. As a useful hint it is worth remembering that most women do not like the clitoris to be stimulated too directly, by rubbing with the finger, for example, as it is so sensitive. Three of the many possible alternatives to such direct stimulation with the fingers are to use the tongue to lick around the clitoris and lips of the vagina, to stimulate the clitoris with the fingers through the protective covering of the vaginal lips or to stimulate to one side or the other of the clitoris. It will, of course, be necessary for her to express how she likes her clitoris stimulated – whether fast or slow, firmly or gently. So far as the woman's stimulation of her male partner is concerned, when stimulating the penis and scrotum she should bear in mind that the very tip of the penis is usually the most sensitive area. If she uses her mouth then she may be able to stimulate the end of the penis more easily than by using her fingers. An alternative to oral stimulation is to stimulate the shaft of the penis below the tip and to caress the scrotum, tops of thighs and perineum, the stretch of skin between the scrotum and the anus. Vary the pace and location of stimulation and remember that caressing the neck, chest, tops of thighs and buttocks may be equally important in sexual arousal as caressing the genital areas.

You will probably notice during these activities that indirect approaches to the genital areas, where you stimulate, for instance the thighs or buttocks and occasionally tease the genitals themselves, may result in a good deal of arousal. This, if it occurs, can be a good indication that you should progress slowly to the genital areas and give a good deal of attention to stimulation of other areas of the body. You should not abandon this playful approach to sexual arousal, if it produces mutual pleasure, in moving on to the later stages. It can be a vital asset in keeping your pre-coital play fresh and exciting.

Insertion of the penis into the vagina is considerably easier after you have both become sexually aroused – the woman having become lubricated and receptive and the man erect. One useful position to use when learning to control tension and anxiety is for the man to lie on his back with legs outstretched and for the woman to adopt a kneeling position above him, her thighs and calves placed either side of his body with her knees pointing towards his armpits. In this position she can raise and lower her vagina over her partner's penis very easily and freely. He, in turn, can remain relaxed and at ease while his penis is inserted into her vagina. In this position, a relaxed one for both partners, confidence in the ability to control sexual arousal may be gained very rapidly. The man should indicate when he is approaching orgasm and, if he wants to delay orgasm, the woman can simply remove her vagina from around his penis by straightening her knees. She can continue to caress him around his body and, when he is again under control, can reinsert his penis and continue as before. In this position the man can also caress his partner's body in those areas which arouse her sexually. Gradually both partners can learn to arouse one another and to control their build-up to orgasm. If you have experienced any sexual tensions and anxieties this position may usefully be practised over a number of days before experimenting with other positions. Of paramount importance is the ability to relax and rest, if this becomes necessary, during foreplay and coitus. Do not *force* yourself to behave in a controlled way; the way to gain control in sex is to change the pace of stimulation, resting from direct genital stimulation when you become too sensitive or too near orgasm and then to rest while, perhaps, talking or caressing the less sexually sensitive areas of the body.

Mental strategies

Under this heading we shall include not only attitudes towards, and knowledge about, sexual behaviour but also skills of communication between partners. Although this might be considered as primarily a physical skill, it is included under the mental strategies heading since it is so closely linked to mental attitudes and desires.

(*i*) *Accepting your inner desires:* If you have been able to discover, either through masturbation or your experiences with your partner, which sexual activities you most enjoy it is important to be able to *accept* your inner desires rather than to pretend that they do not exist or that they are less desirable than some other activities. It may be of great help here to sit down, on your own, and write down some of the things which you have previously, perhaps only very fleetingly, allowed yourself to think about. In writing down these desires you will take them outside your mental environment and put them into the completely new context of the outside world. Here they may be seen in a completely new perspective so that they are no longer as outlandish or unacceptable as they were while confined to your *cerebral cortex*. With this list started you may then find that you are able to express yourself progressively more easily on paper and include details about the activities involved. You may even be able to embellish on them now that you have acknowledged their existence.

(*ii*) *Communicating your desires:* Next it is important that these personal preferences are communicated to your partner. This will be especially useful, and made considerably easier, if your partner has at the same time been preparing a similar list. You should then both find some relaxed time, possibly during one of your periods of caressing, when you can begin to discuss these ideas, which have already been made less anxiety producing because they have been written down. At this point a further advantage of writing down your desires is that if verbal communication proves to be too embarrassing you can begin the communication by exchanging your written lists.

(*iii*) *Do not force yourself:* Now that communication has begun, the last and very important stage in mental communication strategies is to ensure that while you have explained your desires and sexual wishes your partner should in no way feel *obliged* to fulfil them.

In the area of attitude shaping and communication you should allow developments to occur slowly, taking some shared desire or non-stressful demand as a starting point. Requests for oral sex, for instance, may provide your partner initially with anxiety and the issue should not be forced. Instead allow gradual exploration and progress towards giving and obtaining each other's desired behaviours by allowing the behaviours to be emitted and then reinforcing them with a piece of behaviour desired by your partner.

Finally you should remember that slow progress towards having all your desires fulfilled should not be thought of as frustrating or failing. On the contrary, it is more likely to ensure that your repertoire is a continually expanding one with the occasional inclusion of new or surprise pieces of behaviour to keep interest and excitement alive.

3 Crisis tactics

The following tactics may be useful in situations where sexual activities have become stressful and are rapidly deteriorating. They will be useful to stop things from getting worse but should be considered only as a kind of behavioural 'band-aid'. As soon as the negative spiralling has been halted you should move quickly to long-term planning to establish a more enjoyable repertoire of sexual behaviour.

Physical skills

Both you and your partner should learn, together, the skills of deep and quick relaxation. You should practise together, perhaps lying side by side on or in bed where, as well as experiencing the highly pleasurable response of relaxation you will also be in close proximity. In this way you will begin to associate pleasurable responses of relaxation with being in your partner's presence.

At the same time your second major aim should be to remove the stress of sexual demand from your physical proximity by instituting a mutual agreement that you will not attempt to arouse each other in a directly sexual way for the time being. When you have developed the ability to relax quickly in one another's presence by removing stressful demands, you should then begin to re-learn patterns of behaviour appropriate to the initial stages of a sexual encounter. A useful exercise here is to relax together and then to take turns in giving one another a massage, perhaps using some pleasantly perfumed oil. You should remember your mutual agreement not to rush towards sexual arousal but just be content to massage one another and to experience the pleasure of being massaged.

Mental strategies
If you are finding it difficult to discuss the problem with your partner then do not try too hard to do so at this stage. In fact at both the physical and mental communication level you should stop trying too hard at all. Doing so will simply serve to take the spontaneity from the situation and will make it dull and irritating. In order that you do not become excessively analytical and merely talk about the problem and your failings, you should concentrate much more on carrying out the crisis physical behaviours outlined above. A new mental attitude will usually develop from this more relaxed physical approach. Since you may not be able to discuss your problems and needs at present with your partner you should make notes for your own benefit when situations arise that provide you with problems. You should note what occurs and what you would have preferred in the situation. Then, when you have collected a reasonable amount of data you can, perhaps, show your partner your notes, as we suggested earlier, and begin a behavioural analysis of your situation. This in itself may provoke the sort of verbal communication which is so necessary.

4 Long-term behaviour modification

After using the Fourteen-Day Programme to learn the basic skills of behaviour change, carry out an analysis of your sexual responses in the way described in Part Three of this book. The questions at the start of this section should have given you some insights into the type of problem which you and your partner experience. As in the Fourteen-Day Programme, baseline data should be recorded under the headings:

Stimulus – the environment in which the behaviour takes place.
Response – what you did.
Consequence – how you or others reacted to what you did.
'*What I would like to have done*' – your desired behaviour under those circumstances.

See Example Four.

Structuring a pathway of sub-goals
In Example Four the following pieces of inappropriate behaviour could be occurring:

1 Inability to forget previous stressful sexual encounters or, possibly, frictions in the marriage.

2 Inability to discuss the situation with partner and so make own anxieties and desires known.

3 Inability to unwind from general life stresses and concentrate attention on sex.

The sub-goals towards the overall goal of enjoying a more relaxed sex life might be arranged as follows:

1 Relaxation exercises carried out with partner.

2 Setting aside a period of time each day which can be devoted entirely to discovering, by talking and caressing, what your partner enjoys.

3 Gradually guiding your own and your partner's words and actions so that you are both receiving maximum pleasure while remaining completely at ease with one another. Progress should be made slowly and at this point no excessive demands should be made.

4 Stimulation of the sexual areas leading gradually to orgasm if either partner should desire it.

5 Including insertion of the penis into the vagina by using a relaxed position (as described earlier) for both partners.

6 Remembering to caress your partner and show other expressions of affection after coitus has been achieved.

7 Developing a general atmosphere of sensuality in your relationship so that sexual encounters will be uninhibited.

Example four – Typical entry on day one of monitoring

Life area: B – Family, marriage, sex and intimacy

Goal: 'I would like to be able to enjoy a more relaxed sexual relationship with my wife'

Behaviour to be monitored: Responses before, during *and after* sex

Stimulus	Response	Consequence	'What I would like to have done'
9.00 p.m. Lounge at home. Wife and self listening to hi-fi. She sitting on sofa, I sitting in armchair away from her. Look at her and feel a surge of desire. Think that it would be enjoyable to go to bed early.	Suddenly felt a twinge of anxiety when I remembered that this occasion might follow the pattern of the last few weeks where I had had difficulty getting a good erection. Did nothing and continued to listen to the music until it was too late in the evening to make love as there would be the pressure of getting up early the next morning.	Felt relieved that would not have to face the possibility of failure again. But later was disappointed that I had not had sex.	Told Jean how attractive and sexy she looked. Moved onto the sofa and begun to pet in an affectionate fashion, then to have gone on to love-making while remaining relaxed and not concerned as to whether or not I would get a good erection.

The reinforcers in this sort of programme are almost always built in to the behaviours concerned. Sexual arousal and pleasurable bodily feelings themselves are powerful reinforcers of behaviour. However, it is often useful to go on to some further enjoyable activity after each period of sexual behaviour during the programme. Remember that it might be fun to take a bottle of wine to bed with you and to lie drinking it in a relaxed way after love-making. Going out for a stroll afterwards may be equally romantic and enjoyable. Bringing your partner breakfast in bed could be yet another way of reinforcing the behaviour. Try to be imaginative with your reinforcers in sexual situations and to make them extensions of the physical pleasures which you have just enjoyed.

Summary

Enjoying relaxed and uninhibited sex is a piece of naturally occurring behaviour which is often blocked by learning processes. By using these same processes in a structured manner, however, the inappropriate physical and mental barriers may be overcome.

To enjoy sexual activity regularly and fully you can conveniently think of it as a type of skill which can be developed. This skill is an open-ended one which you can continue to expand during a complete lifetime.

Goal two – 'I would like to be able to enjoy a better relationship with my children'

There are two main periods of their lives during which children's behaviour changes markedly in step with changes in their development. The first is during the period of infancy up until about the age of eight or nine years when the child is acquiring the rudiments of social behaviour. Research has shown that it is in these early years that many important changes occur. The way in which they relate to brothers, sisters and parents during this period provides a rich opportunity to mould the child's development. The second occurs during puberty when the child is beginning to grow away from the immediate family in anticipation of their independence. At this stage the behaviours being acquired are those of relationships with members of the opposite sex, the development of a future career, decisions about where to live and the building up of a lifestyle outside the home environment. At this time the parent may appear to the child variously as repressive, helpful, informative, guilt-producing and in a variety of other, probably swiftly changing roles.

During both of these stages of development parents are able, by use of the principles of positive reinforcement, to help their children to develop their most appropriate lifestyle. To do this, however, it is necessary to act as far as possible as a developer of potential and of the child's own ideas and behaviours, rather than as the agent who initiates those ideas. In other words the parents must be able to observe very accurately the way in which the child is developing under their own efforts, to extract behaviours which seem meaningful to the child and then to make suggestions on their further development. In doing this, however, the parents should take care that they do not simply attempt to fulfil at second hand some wish which has been suppressed in their own lives. Such channelling is quite likely to lead to vocational and personal difficulties for the child who may later be in conflict over whether he or she should follow their own ambitions or carry out their parents' wishes.

If a child *has* been wrongly channelled, the problems which can arise during the first period of development include school-refusing, bed-wetting and tantrums. This may often be due to a lack of aptitude or interest in the areas into which the child is being directed. For this reason you would do well to assess your child's progress every few months during this period to find out whether they are interested in their educational pursuits and social development and, if not, how you might help them to be more content. In adolescence, discontent brought about by inappropriate channelling might lead to resentment and rebellion, often ill-defined, against parents.

1 Identifying areas of difficulty

In order to clarify any areas of difficulty in your child's life or in

158

your relationship with your child you should complete the following ten statements by selecting one, or both, of the alternatives given which most closely reflect your child's or your own behaviour in a similar situation.

1 When my young child cries or has a temper tantrum for no really good reason

(a) I rush to give attention knowing that I can quieten him quickly and get back to my work. (b) I shout at him to be quiet and go and find something to do.

2 When my young teenage child asks if he or she can stay out late some evenings

(a) I say yes and give in because he or she would sulk for days. (b) I tell him or her to make up their own mind.

3 When my adolescent child talks about the sort of career to follow

(a) I agree with their suggestions so as not to start an argument. (b) I tell them to think about it and leave it at that.

4 If my child feigns illness to stay away from school

(a) I call the school and make an excuse to save any trouble later. (b) I just let them run around all day while I am at work.

5 If my children ask to talk to me, for instance about sex or school-work

(a) I ask them to talk to my spouse later on. (b) I buy them a book to read on the subject.

6 If I discovered that my child had been having sexual relationships

(a) I would keep him or her in during the evening over the next few weeks. (b) I would let it continue and let them solve their own problems.

7 If my children are fighting

(a) I run out immediately and spend some time calming the situation. (b) I let them carry on or just shout at them to be quiet.

8 If my children start taking an interest in smoking, drinking or taking drugs

(a) I keep them in at nights and away from temptation. (b) I let them carry on and take no notice.

9 If my child seems to have no interest in a career or school-work
(a) I do not press the issue in case they may become angry and
hostile. (b) I let them drift along hoping that some interest
will develop.

10 If my child asks to do something, go somewhere or follow
some interest which would involve effort and expense or
leaving their usual studies
(a) I would say no to the demands. (b) I would say that if they
could find the means then it was OK.

If you have scored predominantly a's it seems likely that your
methods of dealing with your children are those of short-term
gain for yourself, helpful in easing current demands on you, but
with the possible long-term effect that those demands increase
despite your responses.

If you have scored predominantly b's it seems likely that your
attitude to your children is one of 'leaving them to their own
devices'. This may get them out of your hair in the short term
but leave them so ill-directed that they become progressively more
difficult to deal with.

If you have a mixture of both a's and b's then probably your
method of bringing up your children is one which swings between
periods of trying to keep them in order and periods of feeling
helpless and letting them simply get on with whatever they want
to do.

2 Skills and strategies

(*i*) *Giving attention to your children:* Talk to your children frequently and give them attention at times when they are not presenting you with any problems. These are the occasions on which
they should receive your attention as you can then work out the
answers to their problems in advance. Further, if you only talk to
your children and discuss important issues with them at a time of
crisis then they will come to feel that they can only approach at
such times. This may lead to the development of attention-seeking
behaviour where they create crisis situations because they have
learned that they then are able to talk to you. Such attention-

seeking behaviour is often an underlying cause of delinquency.

(*ii*) *Using 'time out' from reinforcement:* It will be obvious from your experiences during the Fourteen-Day Programme that you should not give reinforcement immediately after disruptive behaviour has occurred as this will tend to increase it. What may not be so obvious, however, is that verbal or physical punishment, a form of attention, can *also* act as a reinforcer and serve to increase the disruptive behaviour which it was intended to suppress. We suggest that you use, instead, a removal of possible sources of reinforcement as the consequence of your child's disruptive acts. This can be done conveniently by removing the child from the immediate situation as swiftly and impersonally as possible, and putting him or her into a spare room with no toys or objects which might be damaged. This is usually called a 'time out' room and that name can be used with the child.

The child should be kept in that 'time out' room, until the tantrum has disappeared, with no comment from the parent. It is probable that the child will create a considerable disturbance the first few times this happens but, as long as you do not weaken, they will quickly understand that the 'time out' room is the only way in which their environment responds to such behaviour. Gradually the undesirable behaviour will diminish until it is no longer a problem.

While this may appear to be somewhat punitive it must be emphasised that the 'time out' room itself should in no way be punishing, certainly *not* a cupboard or cellar, but simply neutral. The child should be left there until he or she becomes quiet. It is important to note that the first response of the child to 'time out' from reinforcing situations is likely to be a marked worsening of the delinquent behaviour. This is inevitable as it has become a pattern to receive reinforcement, in terms of parental intervention and attention, for such behaviour. Greater efforts will therefore be made to obtain that accustomed reinforcement. However, with continued effort the child's behaviour will soon come under control.

When using 'time out' procedures it is very important to notice when the child is carrying out appropriate and constructive behaviour and to reinforce such patterns either by simply talking and showing your interest in what is going on, or by doing something which you know your child enjoys.

(*iii*) *Sexual development:* If your child is expressing interest in sexual activity you should prepare yourself to answer questions on the subject. The information contained in the two other goals in this life area may be helpful here. It is not necessary or even advisable to force-feed children with the facts of life. If, for example, you go into detailed description of unusual sexual acts, when the child has only asked where babies come from, they are unlikely to be able to absorb the information anyway. The questions should be answered naturally and without hesitation. In this way you will reinforce their questioning behaviour and, when they are ready to absorb more detailed information, they will come back and ask for it. You should of course make it clear that they are at liberty to do so at any time. You should remember that children mature at different rates and will discover their own feelings of sexuality at different ages.

(*iv*) *Drink, drugs and sex:* If the child wants to smoke, drink, take drugs or experiment with sex, a useful strategy is to confront them with your concern. You should discuss their feelings with them and find out whether there is any pressure on them to perform in this way, in which case they might need support from you to resist that pressure, or whether they feel a need to experience these things in order to satisfy their curiosity.

In this case it is essential to let them know that they can come back to you at any time if difficulties have resulted from their experimentation. You must on no account adopt a repressive attitude which closes the lines of communication. If things go wrong, be there to help them sort out the problems in a non-judging way and to support your child through the readjustment which may come. However, bear in mind that giving advice on contraception may be much less traumatic if your child is experimenting sexually than helping, for example, to obtain an abortion or receiving a paternity suit.

(*v*) *Dealing with requests:* Do not simply reject a child's request out of hand. Neither should you accede to a request in such a way that the child feels guilty about asking. If you have difficulties in agreeing to a request tell your child so, together with your reasons for those difficulties, and ask your child to think about the reasons for the request for a little while longer.

(*vi*) *Adolescent rebellion:* If your child is rebelling in adolescence to a degree which you find almost intolerable, do not feel that you must put up with this behaviour for fear of being considered an oppressive parent. Discuss the situation with the child and make it clear that your life is becoming very difficult. In this instance you might try and form a contract with your child in which you agree to do certain things in return for their agreeing to behave in a certain way on difficult issues. In this case you might encourage your teenage child to read this book in order to gain insight into the problems and to devise methods of controlling them.

(*vii*) *Answering questions:* Always discuss your children's problems with them immediately they are presented to you. Do not hedge and avoid the issue because you have not the time or feel too tired. Give the best advice you can, but if you do not know some facts or feel you do not have the experience to deal with a problem be prepared to say so and find out.

3 Crisis tactics

Physical skills

In the face of a crisis relaxation training may be an important skill in achieving a calm approach to the situation. At times of stress during a family trauma, both children and parents may benefit greatly from intensive relaxation training. This will remove some likelihood of the event being turned into an indelible and anxiety producing memory. We know that the greater the anxiety in a situation the more likely a lasting phobia is to develop. To take some of the steam out from the fraught situation may be of long-term benefit to the child.

Mental strategies

If you are presented with a sudden crisis by your children try not to be judging or shocked. Even in such extreme situations as a little girl being assaulted sexually by a man, it has been observed that any obvious signs of distress tend to come after the parents and police have been questioning her for a considerable time. The child herself, unless physically injured, may not have been too disturbed about the incident but the furore and attitudes of adults afterwards can prove traumatic and damaging. This is not to say that such incidents and less obviously disturbing ones should be ignored when they occur, but it is important not to allow excessive emotion to enter into the discussion and later adjustments but to treat the situation in as firm, kind and calm a way as possible.

4 Long-term behaviour modification

Long-term planning should be instituted immediately after a crisis, as quickly as possible. Goals for dealing with the situation should be set up over a period of time. First of all you, your spouse and your children should take the Fourteen-Day Programme and carry out the Seven-Day Analysis, keeping records of the actual family situations which provide baseline data which should be listed under the following headings:

Stimulus – the environment in which the behaviour takes place.
Response – what you did.
Consequence – how you or others reacted to what you did.
'*What I would like to have done*' – your desired behaviour under those circumstances.

See Example Five.

Structuring a pathway of sub-goals
In the above example the following pieces of inappropriate behaviour can be observed:

1 Inability to remain calm and keep temper under control at difficult times.

2 Inability to relax while the family is causing a disturbance.

3 Inability to communicate with the children in terms which they can understand and relate to.

The following sub-goals might be used to overcome these particular difficulties, in a behaviour modification programme:

164

Example five – Typical entry on day one of monitoring

Life area: B – Family, marriage, sex and intimacy

Goal: 'I would like to be able to enjoy a better relationship with my children'

Behaviour to be monitored: Own and children's responses during communication difficulties

Stimulus	Response	Consequence	'What I would like to have done'
5.50 p.m. Sitting in lounge when suddenly hear scream from five-year-old child in the kitchen.	Rush to the kitchen and shout at the boy asking why he is screaming for no reason.	Screaming stops briefly but began again 15 mins later.	Ignored the screaming and relaxed, then go and speak to the child when he is quiet and playing.
11.30 p.m. Sitting at home waiting for fifteen-year-old daughter to arrive home. She has been staying out late with her boyfriend recently. Daughter arrives.	I demand angrily to know where she has been since she has not been home for the whole evening.	She bursts into tears and rushes off to bed without answering. I feel angry and humiliated.	Kept my temper. Asked her if she had had a good evening. Gently steered the conversation around to my concern about her being out late and discussed it from there.

1 Establishing baseline data for the boy's temper tantrums.

2 Learning relaxation methods for lowering own levels of tension when problems arise.

3 Finding a room in the house where the child can be taken for 'time out' if he continues with his attention-seeking behaviour.

4 Using reinforcement with the younger child to increase periods of constructive behaviour.

5 Establishing and persevering with a programme of 'time out' and reinforcement.

6 Establishing baseline data to determine how often and for how long your daughter stays out late. With the facts written down the situation may not be as bad as you previously thought. It also gives facts to discuss with your daughter when carrying out the next sub-goal.

7 Asking if you and your daughter can talk as adult to adult at some time convenient for her. Fix a time and stick to it yourself. At that meeting voice your own anxieties about her being out so late.

8 Asking your daughter if she would like to discuss anything about her life at present with you. Self-disclosure can be useful here, giving your daughter some insight into some of the problems you might have had in your own life and the worries encountered.

9 Being open-minded if she discusses her boyfriends and other relationships. Being non-judging and expressing your interest in meeting any of her friends at any time.

10 Being comforting and supportive if it seems that she is having difficulties in her relationships, perhaps of a sexual nature, or has become involved with drugs or alcohol. Finding out whether she would like your help in either re-establishing herself with her friends on a different footing or leaving their company for others.

11 Leaving an avenue well open to you for her to keep you informed of how things are going.

12 Reinforcing good communication each time she comes back to tell you how things are going in this area by thanking her for having confidence in you and generally treating her with respect and social acceptance.

The reinforcement which you will obtain from carrying out these sub-goals will usually be integrated with the more productive and satisfying relationship which you are developing. Be sure to notice this more satisfying situation and keep it at the front of your thoughts when considering your overall family relationships.

Summary

Enjoying a good relationship with your children involves learning to make compromises and to interact with as little friction as possible. It is unrealistic to consider that such a state of affairs should occur spontaneously.

When physical and communication barriers arise to prevent such enjoyable relationships, learning principles can be used to overcome these obstacles and to build up the skills necessary to enjoy successful and rewarding interactions with your children.

Goal three – 'I would like to be able to get on better with my marriage partner'

Although in most marriage ceremonies a contract is formed between two people to live together harmoniously for the rest of their days, there is never any explicit teaching as to how this happy state can be obtained. Indeed, there seems to be the feeling before a marriage that people are either 'suited' or 'unsuited' to one another. After a few years, they are said to have either a 'good marriage' or a 'bad marriage'. In other words the whole concept of marriage tends to be looked upon rather like buying a second-hand car: as something which either works or not depending on the luck of the draw. In fact if we look at the 'good marriage', we can see that the couple's behaviour involves a set of highly developed learned skills dealing with close interpersonal relationships. The couple themselves may be unaware that they have gradually acquired certain necessary skills over a period of time. These skills include compromise, communication, assisting with the spouse's problems, coping with the spouse's needs, making up after rows, sharing the chores and duties, being mutually supportive in public and in private and keeping their interests varied.

167

Our approach for dealing with marital problems is based upon the development of such skills. It is not helpful simply to diagnose a marriage as bad. We need to look carefully, day by day, at detailed records of interactions between the marriage partners in order to establish when and under what circumstances pieces of behaviour damaging to the relationship occur.

Even in the 'bad marriage' there is often quite a lot of good. Usually, in a marital breakdown, the good features of the marriage suffer a halo effect from those aspects which go wrong. For instance, the fact that his wife has worked hard during the evening to get the children to bed and enable the two of them to have some time together, may be completely ignored by the husband who has earlier in the evening listened to his wife's complaints about a plumbing fault which he promised, but forgot, to put right. The halo effect operates in his remembering how resentful he felt about his wife's complaints earlier in the evening and still feeling annoyed when she is handing out behaviour which he desires.

Because of this he may remain irritated even though he could relax in his wife's company.

Similarly, the wife who gets flowers from her husband when he returns from work may still be angry over an argument that morning. Because of this she may dismiss the gift ungraciously rather than accept it as a peace offering.

In both these examples positive behaviours are being carried out in marriages which might be termed bad. We are saying here that there are likely to be some positive features in almost every marriage. These can be used as building blocks from which to develop a satisfying relationship.

1 Identifying areas of difficulty

In order to clarify any areas of difficulty in your marital relationship you should complete the following ten statements by choosing one, or both, of the alternatives given which most closely reflect your behaviour in a similar situation.

1 On my way home from work/at the time when my partner is due to return home from work

(a) I become increasingly withdrawn and anxious about the evening ahead. (b) I become irritable and negative about the evening ahead.

2 When my partner addresses a 'ridiculous' remark or question to me
(a) I become upset and downhearted that he/she should have to talk to me like that. (b) I feel contemptuous and too bored even to bother answering.

3 If I have had a row with my partner
(a) I become depressed and concerned about the marriage breaking up. (b) I refuse to allow that I was wrong to any degree and would rather not talk to my partner for days than be the first to give in.

4 In a group with my partner on social occasions
(a) I feel afraid to say what I want in case my partner disapproves. (b) I become embarrassed and derisive about my partner's conversation.

5 When discussing my problems with my partner
(a) I am concerned that my partner might think them trivial and unworthy of discussion. (b) I soon drop the conversation as it is clear that there is no interest on my partner's side.

6 When I feel that my partner wants a row about something
(a) I make excuses to leave the situation as I find rows frightening. (b) I think 'To hell with this – I'll make sure I give as good as I get, and better.'

7 If I think of my partner starting a relationship with somebody else
(a) I become very upset and anxious. (b) I would look for an opportunity to start such a relationship first.

8 I would like to find some outside interest which would take me away from the house for a few evenings a week but
(a) I am frightened that my partner will feel I am no longer interested in the marriage. (b) I know my partner would not only fail to support me in the venture but also deride it.

9 In discussing financial matters with my partner
(a) I am ill at ease and anxious in case I am criticised. (b) I feel

169

that I am simply being manipulated by my partner's continued thoughts about money.

10 When my partner gives me a gift
(a) I feel that the money could have been spent on more necessary items. (b) I immediately suspect that something is being covered up or that I am being bought off.

A predominance of a's in your scoring will indicate that you, and perhaps your partner also, experience a good deal of anxiety about your relationship continuing. You are probably on edge for a good deal of the time wondering how your actions have been interpreted and what will transpire as a result of them. You may become upset over minor criticisms and be too sensitive about your partner's behaviour.

A predominance of b's will indicate that you feel a good deal of contempt for and boredom with your partner and, probably, the feeling is returned. Your repertoire of behaviour has possibly become stilted and stereotyped, but you feel unable to change this for fear that any suggestion on your part will be received in the usual disdainful way.

A mixture of a's and b's might indicate that you are in a situation where you feel bored, unfulfilled and anxious about the marriage breaking down.

2 Skills and strategies

The major building blocks on which a fulfilling marriage may be constructed are those of physical relief from stress and an ability to think of your marriage as one which might be open to improvement while being able to discuss the ways in which it may be improved with your spouse.

The following skills and strategies will be helpful in developing a programme.

(*i*) *Dealing with rows:* The ability to wind up a row quickly and begin talking and interacting again in a productive way is a vital marriage skill. A set of two or three major strategies can be developed by which to end the row. For example, you may decide, during moments of harmony, to invent a private joke which signals a truce. The rule must be observed every time and both partners must stop arguing at once at that point and make up very positively or simply carry on about their normal routine.

(*ii*) *The positive value of rows:* It is important to argue, when necessary, over important issues. In some marriages the partners never row because they are terrified of the possible irreparable damage to their relationship. In such cases, communications are blocked and small discontentments are allowed to smoulder beneath the surface so that when they do erupt they are completely out of proportion. This couple has to learn to argue in a controlled way in order to practise rowing and later making up.

(*iii*) *Considering the other's viewpoint:* Although in many instances the feelings and sentiments of your partner may appear trivial or even inconsiderate, it is useful to be able to understand their statements and questions by trying to see what they mean from *their* point of view. A useful method of accomplishing this is for the couple occasionally to reverse their roles – the husband to argue the wife's point of view and the wife to argue on behalf of the husband. A row or discussion carried out in this way may quickly lead to insights for both partners in what went wrong for the other.

(*iv*) *Reinforcing your partner:* The ability to reinforce or reward pieces of desirable behaviour which your partner has carried out positively will lead to their future repetition. Even though previously they may have carried out some behaviour which is displeasing, it is important to be able to take a positive and possibly very small behaviour pattern and to reinforce it so that it can be encouraged.

(*v*) *Being supportive in company:* In social situations it is most important for your partner to feel that they have your support. It is damaging to pick holes in their conversation or to be pedantic about what they are saying. It is much more valuable either to lend weight to their arguments or to look as though you are listening attentively to it. Do not pounce on each small slip which your partner may make but rather encourage them. An arm around the waist is often invaluable, as might be a small squeeze or hug from time to time.

(*vi*) *Accentuate the positive – eliminate the negative:* Store up pleasant memories of your partner which you can later recount and relive together – for instance, a good sexual experience, a good holiday, a pleasant dinner party and so on. In the 'bad marriage' this skill is often displaced by storing up the faults and mistakes of the other and using them as ammunition in arguments.

Accept your partner and your partner's feelings at face value. In many marriages the demands which partners put upon one another to change their basic personalities drastically place excessive stresses on the relationship. Extract from your partner's behaviour those facets which you find attractive and when they occur follow them by reinforcing behaviour of your own.

(*vii*) *Forming a contract with your spouse:* Bearing in mind that the 'good marriage' is a collection of skills of interaction, it is necessary to consider how this set of skills might be built up. Like all skills it will have to go through a formal acquisition stage before it becomes second nature – much like the actions of driving a car or using a typewriter. It will be necessary in order to do this, to produce a list of responses which you would have preferred your spouse to have made in situations where they have, in your opinion, been unjust or punishing. We will show you in the Long-Term Modification planning how to gather such data. For the purposes of illustration, however, let us consider a typical list of behaviours which a husband and wife have produced for those situations where the desired behaviour might not have been forthcoming from their spouse. This short list, to which another couple of requirements may be added every few days as the records are kept, may form the basis now of a partnership reinforcement contract. Both partners agree that if either of them carries out one of the behaviours desired by the other, then this will be reinforced by responding with behaviour which the other desires. For example, if the husband in the above situation comes in from the office and is allowed ten or fifteen minutes to wash and unwind, he should reinforce being allowed his privacy by going to his wife and immediately chatting about her day. Similarly if the wife receives half an hour of help with the chores from her husband, she might reinforce this by asking him if he wants to go down to the local with

Man	Woman
'*I would like . . .* ten minutes on my own to wind down when I come home from work.'	'*I would like . . .* fifteen minutes of conversation with my husband before the evening meal following my day at home with the children.'
a cuddle in front of the fire during the evening.'	half an hour's help with the chores from my husband to give me a little free time in the evening.'
being sent off happily by my wife on my one night out in the week.'	being given a surprise outing to the cinema or restaurant now and again.'
sex in the evening when it is clear from my behaviour earlier that I am feeling in the mood.'	some expression of appreciation of my cooking, the way the house looks, and my appearance.'
to have something unusual prepared for me to eat when I come home at night.'	on occasions when I do not feel like sex, just to have a cuddle in an affectionate way.'

his friends or she might cuddle him. In other words, whenever either partner notices a piece of behaviour in the other which they find positive this should be reinforced by carrying out one of the behaviours desired by the other partner. The contract can be gradually expanded until you find yourselves reinforcing one another almost automatically.

In developing these contracts the following points should be observed:

1 Always try to have an equal number of desired behaviours for each partner and maintain that equality as the list increases. Having inequalities is likely to result in resentment since one partner will be getting more from the contract than the other.

2 Do not use the word 'don't'! Never put down a negative desired behaviour, such as 'I wish she would not nag so much', 'I wish he wouldn't go out so much'. Negative behaviours, as we explained earlier, are very difficult to reinforce. Instead you should take the implied positive statement which in these examples might be 'I would like to have a period of thirty minutes when I return from work when we only talk about pleasant things rather than chores or problems', or, in her case 'I would like him to go out on a Tuesday night and try to get back by 11 o'clock and then spend the other nights of the week at home, or going out with me'.

3 Keep the number of items on the contract small to begin with. Between five and ten, depending upon their complexity, is quite enough. You should add new items at about the rate of two per week over the next six to eight weeks.

4 In situations where there is a complete clash (for example, when the husband returns from work he wants to spend the first thirty minutes reading the paper and the wife wants to spend the same period talking about her day) some compromise must be made. If there is more than one such clash then one partner should give way on one issue while the other gives way on another issue. If it is impossible to resolve things in this way then toss a coin to decide.

5 While all these skills may appear artificial at first they will become easier and 'more natural' as time goes on.

6 If your partner refuses to engage in this sort of programme you can still carry it out yourself. It may be more difficult to reinforce their behaviour when you are getting no rewards for yours but you can still reward their positive behaviour selectively. They may then copy your reinforcing behaviour. You might reward your own positive behaviour towards your spouse by allowing yourself a reinforcer as in the Fourteen-Day Programme.

3 Crisis tactics

Physical skills
Since your marital problems will almost certainly be producing high levels of physical tension and anxiety, an immediate step which will reduce these difficulties is to learn how to relax together. You should carry out the relaxation instructions contained in the Fourteen-Day Programme and possibly try to increase their effect by gently stroking and massaging one another during relaxation

periods. If it is not possible to relax together you may still derive a great deal of benefit by using the procedures on your own.

Mental strategies

If you have a lot of unspoken resentment and unfulfilled wishes you should begin to set these down on paper as quickly as possible so that you stop them building up to an intolerable level in your mind. You should further try to express your needs to your spouse as calmly and as unemotionally as you can, together with possible ways in which you might work jointly on them.

In this situation crisis tactics are of limited value as they will generally serve only to cover up more basic and unresolved difficulties. You should, therefore, proceed to a Long-Term Behaviour Modification programme as quickly as possible.

4 Long-term behaviour modification

Preferably both of you should carry out the Fourteen-Day Programme paying particular attention to the three sub-goals of relaxation training, record keeping and reinforcement. Then you should go on to a detailed Seven-Day Analysis of your marital situation, gathering baseline data which you can use for your long-term behaviour modification programme. In this Seven-Day Programme you should both keep records independently of one another, and not show one another your records until the end of this period. Then, however, you should swop records over so that you can see the situations which arose from your spouse's point of view. At this stage you will gain considerable insight into your partner's needs and behaviours. Situations which you thought quite trivial may have been found by your partner as important stresses in your marriage, and vice versa.

Record keeping

The records which both you and your spouse keep should be under the headings of:

Stimulus – the environment in which the behaviour takes place.

Response – what you did.

Consequence – how you or others reacted to what you did.

'*What I would like my spouse to have done*' – the behaviour you desired under those circumstances.

See Example Six.

Structuring a pathway of sub-goals

In Example Six we might identify the following inappropriate behaviours:

1 Inability to reinforce positive behaviour by spouse.
2 Inability to show either positive or negative feelings.
3 Inability to relax with partner.

The following sub-goals might be used in a programme for overcoming these problems:

1 Learn to relax together.

2 Keep records of your own and your spouse's behaviour.

3 Produce a list of behaviours which you would like your spouse to carry out.

4 Exchange your lists and records and discuss them together.

5 Establish a list of reinforcing behaviours which you can use to form the basis of a contract between you.

6 Discuss one or two issues on which your opinions differ and work out a strategy for making up after an argument.

7 Have a full scale argument about a point of difference and make up afterwards.

8 Practise swopping roles when arguing to gain insight into your partner's point of view.

9 Gradually increase the list of desired behaviours which you want from your partner.

10 Even after it has become automatic to carry out your contract you should now and again reassess your marital situation and add one or two more items to the contract.

Reinforcement of behaviour is, as usual, of prime importance in developing behaviours in this goal area. In this case, the reinforcers which you use will be those which have been established in your contract with your spouse, your behaviour will be reinforced by your spouse and vice versa. Gradually, you will also find your own

Example six – Typical entry on day one of monitoring

Life area: B – Family, marriage, sex and intimacy

Goal: **'I would like to be able to get on better with my marriage partner'**

Behaviour to be monitored: Responses by partner in marital situations

Stimulus	Response	Consequence	'What I would like my spouse to have done'
6.00 p.m. Arrive home from work after exhausting day.	Make for the stairs so that I can have a wash and change before joining the family.	Spouse calls up the stairs to ask why I have not contacted the plumber about the blocked sink. I feel angry and resentful but do not feel able to show it.	To be left alone for five minutes while I wash and then to talk when I come down the stairs.
11.00 p.m. In bedroom spouse in bed. I get into bed.	Put arm round spouse and cuddle up.	Have arm pushed away with statement that spouse feels tired and has to be up early in the morning. I become tense and retreat from spouse.	For spouse to turn over and cuddle back, possibly leading to intercourse but not necessarily.

behaviour becoming internally reinforced and so consolidate your new responses.

Summary
The existence of a legal marriage contract does not, of itself, produce a viable relationship. It is necessary to learn the skills of interacting with a spouse and to understand that physical and communication barriers, while they may arise through unfortunate accident, may be removed by learning processes and behavioural contracts. In those marriages which are happy this has occurred by fortunate chance. The use of the techniques described in this section to remove these barriers should not be considered as artificial, they are the building blocks by which every successful marriage proceeds.

Life area C – Social and interpersonal relationships

In this life area we will deal with difficulties and strategies involved in the following commonly expressed goals:
'I would like to be able to . . .

1 control my weight.'
2 make new friends easily and confidently.'
3 make a formal or informal speech fluently.'

Goal one – 'I would like to be able to control my weight.'

In dealing with weight control problems we shall consider the eating behaviours of meal times and snacks and look at the ways in which inappropriate behaviour in either of these areas can lead to problems of overweight. Our programme differs from conventional slimming courses in that while we recognise the importance of sensible, balanced diets, we shall place much greater emphasis on *how* we eat rather than *what* we eat. We shall not be concerned with watching scales for a week by week weight loss so much as with the hour by hour and minute by minute methods of eating. Our aim is to make the overweight person eat like a thin person, for if they can develop the same eating habits as the thin person their weight will not only reduce but stabilise and be maintained. This will overcome the problem of the regaining of weight – a fate which overtakes ninety-seven per cent of overweight people on conventional diets.

1 Identifying areas of difficulty

To help you identify those times at which you might be most at risk from inappropriate eating behaviour and to examine those times at which you most need to develop strategies of 'thin eating', complete the following ten statements by selecting one, or both, of the alternatives given which most closely reflect your own behaviour in a similar situation.

1 When I feel depressed or tense
(a) I make a snack for company. (b) I take second or third helpings at meal times.

2 When I feel frustrated sexually or socially
(a) I make a snack to buck me up. (b) I gorge at meals.

3 When watching TV or listening to the hi-fi
(a) I like a snack for company. (b) I eat a meal from a tray on my lap.

4 On the way to or from work
(a) I have a snack on my journey to relieve the boredom.
(b) I dream about a huge meal that I will have later in the day.

5 When I am eating
(a) I have a snack in my hand while I am doing other things like making a phone call or reading a magazine. (b) I put my plate and utensils on a cluttered corner of a table to eat.

6 While I am in the process of eating
(a) I am ready with my snack poised to take another mouthful as soon as I have swallowed the last. (b) At meal times my fork is always laden with food and never left idly on my plate even for a few seconds.

7 When I think back on the food which I have just eaten
(a) I cannot remember what my snack tasted like. (b) I cannot appreciate the quality of cooking which went into the meal.

8 When drinking with my food
(a) I swill down my snack with coffee or tea before emptying my mouth. (b) I drink at meals with my mouth still full of food.

9 When cooking in the kitchen
(a) I make myself a snack even though I may be eating shortly.
(b) I pick at the dishes before the meal and clear all the remains from the serving plates afterwards.

10 When I eat an item of food such as an apple or bar of chocolate
(a) I cannot resist finishing the whole piece of food during one snack. (b) It is impossible for me to leave part of the meal on my plate at meal times.

If you have scored predominantly a's then a major problem in your eating habits would seem to be concerned with snacks eaten either between or instead of meals. In this case your behaviour modification programme should focus on those times other than set meals when you cannot resist the temptation to eat. This may involve your learning other behaviours which give you similar relief from, for instance, depression or tension, or equal pleasure. Relaxation training may be an effective way of doing this.

If you have scored predominantly b's then it looks as if you lack the necessary strategies to establish 'thin eating' behaviours during meal times. In this case you should practise the skills and strategies which we shall list for bringing eating behaviour under control at set meal times and in company.

A high score in both areas indicates that you are eating in an excessive and inappropriate way at meal times and increasing the overweight problem by between-meal snacks. In this case you should concentrate, of course, on both snack control and meal time control, including both situations in your behavioural analysis charts.

2 Skills and strategies

We have suggested that the ability to control weight effectively must be considered as a skill. As such it may be learned through a knowledge of the ways in which to plan how and where you eat. It is not sufficient simply to subject yourself to a punishing crash diet, since it will not teach you how to maintain the resulting weight loss. In the following strategies we shall explain some of the behaviours which an overweight person might develop in order to eat like a thin person and so become, and remain, slim themselves.

The strategies which we shall explain will be divided into two groups. The first is concerned with your actual eating behaviour and surroundings in which you eat. The second group refers mainly to general readjustments of lifestyle so that you start to think and feel like a slim person while eating like one.

Eating tactics
(i) *Tasting food – the art of sensual eating:* Since the overweight person will, typically, eat food quickly and only keep it for a very short time in the mouth, the tactic of tasting food in detail should be practised. This provides one method by which to obtain choice over whether or not to continue eating a certain food. A useful exercise to carry out daily over the course of a week is as follows:
Take a bar of chocolate and break off one small corner.
Place it on your tongue and draw it slowly into your mouth, smelling and tasting the chocolate as you do so.
Now press the chocolate against the roof of your mouth and hold it there, without swallowing, until it begins to dissolve. Notice how the substance starts to coat your mouth and teeth. Move your tongue slowly around your mouth so that every part is coated with chocolate.
After one or two minutes spent savouring the chocolate in this sensual way (closing your eyes and relaxing in a chair may help this exercise) let the cloying mixture run down your throat, swallowing small amounts at a time.
When you have cleaned your mouth completely, by licking with your tongue, spend some time just remembering the taste and texture of the chocolate.
Now ask yourself: 'Do I want another piece of chocolate?'
If the answer is 'yes' then carry on and repeat the exercise.

But almost certainly the reply will be 'no', as the sensual way in which you have eaten the one, small piece usually satisfies your hunger and craving for the foodstuff.

You can repeat the same exercise with an apple, taking a bite and sucking and licking the portion, then chewing it slowly and sensually before swallowing.

Once you understand how to eat in a sensual way you will appreciate the difference between eating for enjoyment rather than merely to fill yourself up.

(ii) *Slow eating – between bite activity:* If you watch a thin person and a fat person eating you will usually notice that the thin person carries out a much greater amount of activity between each mouthful of food than the fat person. The thin person's learned behaviour patterns take the form of putting food into the mouth, chewing and savouring as described above, swallowing the food, probably putting the knife and fork down for a few seconds, possibly sipping wine or talking briefly to a companion. Then another mouthful may be taken and so on. The fat person will generally tend to follow the pattern of filling the mouth with food, talking, if completely unavoidable, through a mouthful of food, loading the fork up and ready to refill the mouth when it is cleared and swilling down each mouthful of food with drink to clear the mouth quickly for the next portion. In other words, for the thin person, the removal of the mouthful of food to the stomach leads to a learned response of a rest pause before the next mouthful. For the fat person, chewing and swallowing a mouthful of food leads to the response of refilling the mouth as quickly as possible.

The results of these two behaviour patterns are quite different. To appreciate the difference it is necessary to understand how the stomach and gut relay signals concerning need for food to the brain and eating mechanisms. There is a delay of several minutes between your stomach's being comfortably full and your brain appreciating this fact. The fat eater pushes food so quickly into the stomach that by the time the brain has received the message that no more is needed the stomach is already overfull. In the case of the thin eater, the rest pauses, and the fact that it takes several minutes longer for the food to build up in the stomach, mean that the brain has much more chance of receiving a signal that sufficient food has been received in time to stop the eating behaviour. In other words, the longer that you can take to eat a meal, by rest pauses between bites and by generally slowing down the time taken to pass the food through the mouth to the stomach, the more chance there is that you will feel full and satisfied before you have gorged yourself excessively. The overweight person often claims that such slow eating in impracticable. Plates have to be cleared away quickly at the family meal; companions at a business lunch may have finished their main course while you are still eating. However, such situations can be coped with. In the overweight family, for instance, it is dramatically effective to institute the tactic of saying that the last person to finish eating will get a special privilege (but not a second helping!). At the business luncheon a comment can be made that your meal is 'too good to rush'. Slow eating combined with sensual eating will make your meal times much more satisfying as you will change from mere gorging into an enjoyment of the whole process of eating and tasting.

(*iii*) *Leaving without grieving:* In both the above tactics it will be quite obvious that, if you say 'no' to the question: 'Do I want any more chocolate or another bite of the apple?', or if your stomach has signalled that it is full and there is still part of your meal left on the plate, then in order not to carry on to gorging behaviour it will be necessary to make the decision to stop eating. On many occasions this will lead you to waste food. The ability to allow food to be wasted is another major distinguishing feature of the 'thin eater' as opposed to the 'fat eater'. The fat eater will often become very anxious at seeing food left, even to the point of clearing up other people's plates as well as their own. The thin eater will quite happily leave food if sufficiently sated or if there is an item of food which they do not particularly like. As practice in the first few days of learning to eat the thin way, you should quite ruthlessly throw food away if, when you have made the decision to stop eating, there is anything left. Perhaps this suggestion leaves you horrified?

As small children most of us were taught to clean our plates, perhaps being told it was shameful and evil to waste food while others were starving. If scraps were left then anxiety and guilt may have resulted which could only be relieved by making sure that, in future, all the food was eaten. From the principles of negative reinforcement explained in Part One you will see that the behaviour of finishing off every scrap of food may have been firmly established by the resulting escape from anxiety. If, in the future, the child or adult felt anxiety from another source, eating, a learned response leading to the removal of anxiety, might be used as a method of escaping the new source of anxiety. In this way the eating behaviour might occur not in response to hunger, as is desirable, but to a feeling of tension, anxiety, or need for comfort. Remember that whether you shovel the remains of unwanted food into your mouth or the dustbin makes no practical difference to others who may be in need. A donation to a charity would be much more useful.

After you have learned to throw food away without guilt or anxiety then you may begin to save food which has been left over for another meal. However, you should do this only when you are quite confident that you will not find excuses, a few minutes later, to finish off the left-overs. It is for this reason, being so easy to rationalise and argue for the finishing up of left-overs, that you should learn to waste food first.

(*iv*) *Calorie counting:* It is clearly necessary to develop the skill of knowing and estimating the calorie content of the food you eat. While we have said that in this programme we are primarily concerned with *how* you eat food, it is obvious that if you continue to eat types of food which are not very filling but high in calories – such as chocolate, cream cakes and pastries – you will still remain overweight. So, combined with the behavioural eating programme must be a learning programme for assessing calorie content. You should do this, initially, by using a calorie chart and weighing and measuring foods. However, as most people find this to be time-consuming and boring, you should also develop visual methods of estimating calorie values. Each time you weigh food to find out its calorie content note also how large the portion looks and use some standard of your own for comparison. The length of your finger, the size of your hand, the volume of your clenched fist are all useful comparisons. Then when you are in a restaurant and need to assess calorie content you can do so quickly by sight and determine how much of the meal you should leave if you wish to limit your calorie intake.

We advise you to adopt a weekly calorie allowance from one of the many diets based on the calorie counting system and on advice from your own doctor. When you have determined your ideal weekly allowance you should begin your weight control programme by sticking strictly to it. Later as we shall explain in the lifestyle strategies, you will be able to introduce considerable variety to the way in which the total calorie intake allowed is made up.

(v) *Never feel hungry?:* The overweight person hardly ever experiences the feeling of hunger as a physical state. Their stomach rarely rumbles and they seldom feel the gnawing pains which thin people have learned to take as a signal for eating. Instead the overweight person will eat in response to all manner of physical and mental sensations. Some we have mentioned above: tension, anxiety, boredom, depression, excitement. Other associations may be external, for instance making a telephone call, watching television, reading a paper or travelling to work can all act as eating triggers. From what we have said in the early chapters it should be obvious that the thin person eats in response to the *stimulus control* of hunger while the fat person eats in response to a wide variety of other stimulus controls. It is therefore necessary for the overweight person to understand and experience feelings of hunger and to observe the feelings of reduction in hunger when food is eaten. To do this we suggest the following exercise:

Refrain from eating for a much longer period than you would normally go without food.
Notice the gradual development of your hunger, and exactly how this feels in your abdomen.
Now, carry out the sensual and slow eating exercises which we have already described.
After each small mouthful or swallow notice what happens to your feelings of hunger and when these have been reduced to zero, use that point as your stimulus to cease eating.

You will probably be surprised at how little food is actually needed. It may take only four or five mouthfuls while, in other circumstances, you might have swallowed twenty or thirty.

Having learned by this exercise how to carry out your eating behaviour in response only to hunger, it will be necessary for you to learn another response to deal with the feelings of tension and anxiety which you may experience from time to time. If the Seven-Day Analysis indicates that you eat primarily in response to anxiety, frustration, boredom, or similar stimuli then it will be necessary for you to develop other pieces of behaviour to relieve these feelings. Such behaviours will vary according to your needs. Usually relaxation skills will be of great importance. You should learn them according to the instructions given in Part Two. If your problems involve relationships, then it may be advisable to use one of the other programmes in this part of the book to remove difficulties which are the indirect cause of your being overweight. You can run this programme alongside your weight control programme as the two will help one another. For example if you are frustrated because you feel unable to develop social relationships due to your weight problem then a reduction in weight combined with an increase in social skills will reinforce one another and give both the best chance of succeeding.

(*vi*) *Where you eat, what you eat:* As we have pointed out earlier, your eating behaviour may have come under very general stimulus control. You may be eating snacks and meals in all sorts of situations and so associate eating with a wide range of stimuli. In order to control inappropriate eating periods you should establish a fixed stimulus situation in which to eat all your meals. For example meal times at home, whether you are eating alone or with others, should always take place in a specific room of the house and preferably at a table. The table should be laid properly and not hurriedly cleared so that only a small corner is being used. The meals should be served so that there are no second helpings available without having to make a journey to the kitchen or perhaps even having to cook extra food. You should not eat and read or watch TV at the meal table but restrict other activities to conversation and the removal of dishes between each course. In this way you will learn to eat only in certain environments. At work you might eat in a certain room or set a small table at the side of your desk if it is impossible to leave your office to eat. However small the change made in your environment it will be important as you will soon come to associate your new stimulus control with the only time at which you eat.

(*vii*) *Walk off your weight:* While physical exercise is extremely valuable in weight control programmes, it is difficult to give a rigid programme of instruction. Clearly someone with an excess weight of fifteen stone might well suffer fatal heart damage if they began an exercise routine of running up and down stairs daily. It is equally clear that for someone who is only 5 lbs overweight a ten minute stroll may be insufficient exertion. The one form of exercise which is both safe and effective is walking. This is a self-regulating exercise, since the fitter, less overweight person will simply walk further and faster than the severely overweight. When using this form of exercise simply set yourself the target of gradually increasing the amount you walk each day, over a period of a few weeks. (You might follow the behaviour modification programme outlined in Part Two of this book for increasing walking.) Even a small increase in daily walking can contribute greatly to your weight loss. As a guide, if you add an extra ten to fifteen minutes daily to your existing walking period and maintain this consistently, in one year you will use up the equivalent of one stone (14 lbs) weight.

Lifestyle strategies – live thin
Although following the individual tactics outlined above will help you to reduce your weight and keep it under control, it is essential that you gradually incorporate weight control into your everyday life.

(*i*) *Accept the unchangeable – and develop self-image:* As you lose weight and your shape and appearance alter it will become clear that while some aspects of your body are changeable, others remain quite fixed. It is possible to reduce surplus fat around your midriff, thighs and hips, but it is impossible to do anything about the bone structure which makes your hips a certain shape; it is possible to remove dewlap but changing the set of your jaw is impossible. It is necessary when watching your physique alter to understand what you can change, appreciate what you cannot change and accept the difference between the two. In your weight control programme develop your appearance as nearly as possible to your ideal. But resist the temptation to look at features you do not like but cannot alter as this will simply undermine your efforts where positive changes are occurring. Make it a practice to stand naked in front of a mirror every day and look at your body from all angles. Note the good points, and watch how these improve as you follow your programme. Remark on them constantly to yourself. Observe how your stomach is flattening, notice how your buttocks are firming, see how your body is gradually developing a more slender shape.

As these positive changes take place you should accentuate them and increase your confidence in your existing appearance by taking care over the way you dress, style your hair and look after yourself generally. Fat people hate their bodies. You must learn to love yours, you must learn to pamper it and devote time to looking after it. Do not feel that a period spent in bathing, grooming and tending to your appearance is wasted. Set aside a period each day when you can do these things. Look on it as part of your weight control programme.

(*ii*) *Change your social habits:* As your weight and shape change, learn to go into those situations which, previously, you would have avoided through self-consciousness. Begin to hold small parties at your home as well as going to clubs and dances to meet people. In developing a new social life you will reinforce again the efforts which you are making in weight control and make the whole process that much more worthwhile.

(*iii*) *Be assertive when you eat:* Once you have learned the tactics for knowing when to stop eating, and how much you should allow yourself to eat, you should not let yourself be browbeaten or blackmailed into eating extra amounts. The waiter who insists on your accepting all the vegetables in the serving dish, the hostess who implores you to take a second helping must both be answered assertively. They must be told, politely but firmly, that you have enjoyed what you have eaten enormously but that to accept more would be an over-indulgence which might well spoil your present satisfaction.

(iv) *Long-term strategies – coping with overeating:* Remember that everybody overeats from time to time. The biggest difficulty encountered by overweight people on a diet is that if they lapse and over-indulge they become depressed and feel that the programme has failed. This usually leads to their overeating even more. For this reason you should actually programme periods of overeating into your lifestyle and establish times when you can gorge yourself. You should save this quite difficult strategy until you have mastered all the others. But even while you are mastering the early skills you should not let the odd moment of over-indulgence upset your programme. If it happens accept the fact without letting it interfere with your programme. In this way you will avoid the guilt often associated with over-indulgence and be able to come back on to your programme without difficulty. In the long term you should plan any meals at which you think you may overeat in terms of calories by building other meals around the special occasion. For instance, a businessman knows that during the coming week he has two lunches at which he may over-indulge. He should, therefore, cut back on some other meals to allow him to accept the extra calorie intake without going over the agreed figure for the week. A wife might know that she is going out in two weeks' time for a family celebration meal at which she may be tempted to eat and drink too much. Again this can be allowed for by cutting back on other meals before and after the special occasion.

By planning your meals weeks and months ahead in this way you can allow yourself to enjoy dinner parties, and restaurant meals without feeling guilty that you have broken your diet. Do not make the unrealistic attempt never to over-indulge. Accept that over-indulgences will occur so that you can enjoy them. Remember that the best way to deal with temptation is to give in to it – on *your* terms.

(v) *Always consider your choices:* The object of the strategies which we have described is to leave the choice in a programme completely in your own hands. As an overweight person you may have felt that you have had no alternative other than to push food down as quickly as possible, to clean every scrap from your plate or to over-indulge yourself. All these exercises have been designed to place the choice in *your* hands – whether it is at a minute by minute level where you decide and choose whether or not to eat another mouthful at a particular meal or at a week by week level where you can choose on which days you will eat a large amount and on which days you will eat less to compensate. Remember, when planning or executing any of these tactics, to consider this point of choice. If you stop to think and consider your choices the result will usually be that you stop overeating in both the short and the long term.

3 Crisis tactics

This section will not be included in this goal area as it is felt that it is not an approach to be encouraged. Overweight is the result of a long period of learned inappropriate behaviour patterns which should be removed or coped with over a similarly long-term period of relearning.

4 Long-term behaviour modification

Start by going through the Fourteen-Day Programme outlined in Part Two of this book then carry out the Seven-Day Analysis described in Part Three. In determining your baseline data you should try to take a typical week without any special changes in surroundings, such as going on holiday.

From your baseline data discover those times when you are particularly likely to eat snacks or eat excessively at meal times by noting the stimuli to which you respond by overeating. It will be very important in this case to include under the stimulus heading internal moods and feelings as well as external elements in your environment.

Record keeping
As with any other behavioural analysis programme you will record baseline data under the headings of:

Stimulus – the environment in which the behaviour takes place and your mood or feelings at the time.
Response – what you did, how long you took.
Consequence – How you or others reacted to what you did.
'*What I would like to have done*' – your desired behaviour under those circumstances.

See Example Seven.

Structuring a pathway of sub-goals
Your analysis will enable you to establish whether you are most at risk of overeating at meal times or between meals or both. It will also help you to determine whether you eat as a response to stress and anxiety rather than hunger. Barriers to successful weight control can be established from this analysis. From example seven a typical list of inappropriate behaviours might be:

1 Inability to relax and unwind unless overeating.
2 Inability to taste food or discriminate between food which is liked and food which is disliked.
3 Inability to establish a consistent place and time at which to eat each meal.
4 Inability to assess the calorific content of meals.

The sub-goals towards the overall goal of weight control might be arranged as follows:

1 Deep relaxation training.
2 Quick relaxation training.
3 Differential relaxation training.
4 Measuring food for calorific value and learning to assess quantity by eye.
5 Sensual eating.
6 Slow eating alone.
7 Slow eating in company.
8 Assigning particular seats at work or table at home as the only place at which to eat in those particular surroundings.
9 Always preparing the correct amount of food for the meal.
10 Sitting at correctly laid place while eating and concentrating only on eating.

Example seven – Typical entry on day one of monitoring

Life area: C – Social and interpersonal relationships

Goal: 'I would like to be able to control my weight'

Behaviour to be monitored: Time, place and quality of food eaten

Stimulus	Response	Consequence	'What I would like to have done'
Arrive home from work. 5.30 p.m. Wondering what to do in the evening. Friends all out. TV only alternative. Feel bored, depressed and tense.	Thought at once of the bread and cheese which I know is in the kitchen. Decided I needed comforting. Went and ate half a pound of cheese with four large slices of thickly buttered bread. Did not really taste it or notice how much I had eaten until later. Ate while doing odd jobs in the kitchen.	Felt better and quite relaxed by the overeating and knew that if I felt depressed again I could go back for more. No idea how many calories had eaten. Must be a lot.	Decided to spend my evening at home productively by writing several letters which are outstanding. Planned for an evening out with friends later that week.

11 Planning long-term eating strategies.
12 Pampering self and improving self-image.

Practise your own sub-goals using self-reinforcement to estab-lish the different pieces of behaviour as you learned during the Fourteen-Day Programme. You can use a list of minor and major reinforcers, collecting those which are most suitable and practical for the behaviour which you are learning. Remember that you can use a points system of reinforcement if it is not possible to provide an immediate reward. As you become slimmer you will receive more and more meaningful reinforcers such as new clothes, new activities with friends and positive comments about yourself. There is the considerable factor of improvement in health which should follow and lead to much less discomfort in situations where you have to exert energy. However, such reinforcement should be saved until much later on in your programme. To strive for it in the early stages will make your task much too difficult and the reinforcement much too delayed. This is the main reason why conventional diets fail to achieve long-term weight reduction. The reinforcement provided by weight loss is too delayed to establish the slim eating behaviour.

Summary

Developing control over your weight can be looked on as a piece of learned behaviour. Fat people and thin people have learned to eat differently.

In developing weight control it is necessary to eliminate in-appropriate 'fat' eating behaviour and to acquire 'thin' eating habits. To do this you should practise certain exercises designed to help you appreciate your food and eat only when hungry.

Where the problem of overeating is triggered by anxiety, relax-ation may be used to reduce the level of tension instead of resort-ing to overeating. It may also be useful to use one of the other programmes in the social or sexual life areas to remove source of stress.

Goal two – 'I would like to be able to make new friends easily and confidently'

We tend to think, incorrectly, that friendships and new acquaintanceships spring up spontaneously. This happens only rarely. A meeting between two strangers in a social situation involves each in carrying out skilled and complex behaviour patterns in talking and listening. In fact, social behaviour can be seen as a series of skills which, when put together in a flexible way, may result in two people becoming interested in one another to a sufficient degree to wish to continue a relationship.

The two major types of behaviour used in social interactions are *receiver* and *sender* skills. By this we mean the ability to listen and respond to another person's point of view and also to be able to give out our own information and make comment effectively and clearly. Within both these skills two elements operate – verbal and non-verbal communication. These are the conveying of information using the voice pitch and volume, body posture, facial expression and hand and arm movements. When we listen or talk we are receiving and sending a mass of complex information. The impression which we give and receive, depends on the overall mixture. In order to create a well-balanced mixture it is necessary to study the component parts of social interchanges.

1 Identifying areas of difficulty

In order that you can more easily identify barriers which may be restricting your performance in social interactions, complete the following ten statements by selecting one, or both, of the alternatives given which most closely reflects your own behaviour in a similar situation.

1 When I enter a social situation
(a) I feel myself blushing and I become anxious. (b) My mind goes blank and I panic in case I have nothing to say.

2 If I see a group of people holding a conversation and wish to join them
(a) I find myself unable to break into the conversation.
(b) I hesitate to make the point in case it is criticised or ignored.

3 If someone begins to talk to me in a social situation
(a) I get tongue-tied and tense. (b) I cannot follow what they are saying because I am thinking frantically about what I should say myself.

4 When I am asked for my opinion in a social setting
(a) I stammer or blush and mumble an excuse for not answering. (b) I feel I should not pause to think about the point because I may be criticised for hesitating.

5 When I am talking to someone in a one-to-one situation
(a) I have difficulty looking the person in the eyes. (b) I am thinking all the time how I look and appear to them.

6 When I am trying to express myself socially
(a) I speak in a monotonous voice which has hardly any volume. (b) I find I can only keep to my idea and not see the other person's point of view.

7 When I am engaged in any discussion where feelings are concerned
(a) I find it impossible to convey my feelings by facial expression or gesture. (b) I refrain from making a comment in case other people do not understand my feelings.

8 When I suddenly find that I have become the centre of attention
(a) My voice falters and anxiety mounts quickly. (b) I find my mind becomes blank and I wonder if I will be able to continue my point.

9 When I see someone in a party situation with whom I would like to become acquainted
(a) I become tense and too nervous to approach them. (b) I tell myself to wait a little longer in case they feel I am being too familiar.

10 When I wish to develop a relationship to a more intimate degree
(a) I become anxious and eventually have to end the conversation and leave. (b) I am unable to ask for a further meeting in case I am rejected.

If you have scored predominantly a's then a major problem in social situations would seem to be physical tension and anxiety or the inability, probably because of such stress, to express yourself in a non-verbal way. In such cases your behaviour modification programme should include learning relaxation skills, and facial and bodily expression so that you can reduce stress to a manageable level and increase your non-verbal skills. For further details see under the physical skills heading below.

If you have scored predominantly b's then it would seem that you lack the necessary mental strategies to deal with receiving and understanding other people's conversations and information and also have difficulty in putting your own thoughts and feeling coherently in conversation. In this case you should practise the skills listed below under the mental strategies heading.

A high score in both areas indicates that a combination of mental and physical barriers is arising to prevent you from engaging effectively in socialising and making friends. To remove these barriers it will be necessary for you to construct a programme which includes training in both mental and physical skills.

2 Skills and strategies

As we have said, the ability to carry out successful social interactions can be regarded as a skill in its own right. Many people expect to become socially skilled with no particular effort and not surprisingly they find that when faced with a social encounter they are lost for an appropriate response to make to the situation.

Physical skills

At a physical level there are two major types of skill which may be learned to help you cope more effectively with social situations. First of all you can learn how to keep muscle tension low so as to avoid a build-up of anxiety. Secondly you can learn how to be expressive with your face, hands and arms in social situations.

(*i*) *Relaxation and anxiety management:* Most people experience a small degree of anticipatory anxiety when entering new social situations. In limited doses such feelings may be quite useful in acting as a buffer and regulating behaviour in the early stages. If anxiety should build up too high it can prevent the development of more flexible and uninhibited behaviours which might lead to more intimate relationships. If this happens, the level of anxiety must be reduced so that the individual can behave as desired.

The skill of most value here is anxiety management in which the potentially inappropriate response of anxiety is used as a beneficial and appropriate response to trigger socially skilled behaviour. You can learn this skill by perfecting the three types of relaxation training which were detailed in the Fourteen-Day Programme.

1 Deep relaxation enables you to identify small increases in stress which might, previously, have passed unnoticed.

2 Quick relaxation is valuable in settling the autonomic nervous system just prior to going into a social encounter and may be used to stop a build-up of anxiety beforehand.

3 Differential relaxation is most useful in situations where you may feel anxious while your body, and especially the voice, is in use. It enables you to relax your posture and neck muscles so that your voice remains steady and controlled and your mannerisms and gestures stay natural.

When you become experienced at relaxation, and this can be achieved in as little as seven days providing you practise regularly each day, your body will soon learn to respond to muscle tension or anxiety by using it as a signal to relax. In this way if you notice small amounts of anxiety as they occur and switch in the relaxation response, your body will gradually learn to relax automatically when it feels the onset of anxiety.

(*ii*) *Body language:* If we observe a person making a point in a social situation we will see that he uses body position, hand and arm movements and facial expression to emphasise verbal points. Some of the more valuable skills which can be practised are those of eye-to-eye contact, open and questioning expressions, nods and smiles, hand motion and the placing of the body.

You should remember that while eye-contact is essential in a discussion or conversation, too much of it for too long a period of time can become very distracting and stressful. Periods of eye-contact normally lie between two and five seconds, with shorter time periods the closer you are to the other person. Between each period of eye-contact you should glance slightly to one side or the other and then, after a few seconds, give another short burst of eye-contact. As with all the rest of the skills described here you can practise this in front of a mirror. Eye-contact can also be used for signalling that you wish the person to whom you are talking to continue the conversation. Normally this is done by saying your final few words on a point while looking the other person fully in the eyes and then, as you reach the end, dropping the tone of your voice and lowering your eyes. This is usually taken by the other person as an invitation to continue the discussion. While listening to another person it is usually appropriate to give periods of eye-contact, with rest pauses between, as they are talking. Continuous eye-contact, or continuous lack of eye-contact can be, as we have said, distressing.

It may also be much more useful, especially if a person clearly has a point which they want to make without interruptions, to use a nod or a smile to show that you are still following their train of thought. Raising the eye-brows in an enquiring way can be interpreted as a request for clarification or continuation of the point while a straight, open look can indicate that you are intensely interested in their subject. The advantage of using such non-verbal communications is that you can devote all your mental energy to following their train of thought and trying to understand their point of view. At the end of their conversation you will then be in an excellent position to follow their arguments or comments with intelligent ones of your own.

If you want to make a very serious point, or impress your listener then it may be necessary to lean towards your listener while speaking. This can be done by bringing your head and shoulders slightly closer to the other person while remaining standing in the same place. Just two or three inches of movement will lend earnestness to your words and be seen by your listener as an underscoring of your statements. In the same way, the use of your hand to point or gesture firmly after each main part of your argument, or even to count off points on your fingers as you go through them, can be employed to lend weight to your words.

Practise these types of behaviour in front of a mirror. Select those which seem most comfortable to you and experiment with them in social situations. Do not worry if, at first, they seem a little forced and artificial. You will soon enjoy the extra life they bring to your conversation.

(iii) Verbal – voice tone and volume: If you have a tape-recorder you can practise these skills, using it to play back your conversations. Listen to your voice as others hear it. Remember that when you hear yourself speak the feedback you obtain is complicated by the physical structure of your own head and skull and you get a different effect from that which others receive. Try to speak at a level which is appropriate to the size of the room in which you are talking. It is irritating to hold a conversation with somebody who speaks too softly. Speak clearly and not too quickly, but vary the pace of your delivery so that you do not sound monotonous. Try to deliver your words at the rate of about 100–120 a minute. Practise correct breathing while talking, taking in a breath at each natural rest pause. This will be much easier if you have already mastered the relaxation skills. If you are expressing a key point in your argument, emphasise this fact by slightly raising the pitch and volume of your voice. At the end of each sentence let your voice drop slightly but do not let it fade away to a point where it cannot be heard.

Mental strategies
(i) Observing social interactions: If you find it difficult to break down social behaviour into the components we have described, try going into social situations and not speaking or interacting but simply observing other people. See if you can spot how the person who is the centre of attraction gets there, by body language, and voice projection. See how he or she maintains this position, being able to carry on talking even though the material is running a little thin. Watch for the way in which some people can tell a story and keep the attention of their audience by not making it too long or involved. Try to decide at what point you could have entered the conversation yourself and what strategies you would have used. In general take off all the demands to perform and simply relax and watch others at work.

(*ii*) *Answering questions:* If you are suddenly confronted with a request for your opinion, never be afraid to say – 'Now let me see if I have that point correctly' or 'Let me think about that for a second.' Ultimately, never be afraid to state that it is a point which you have never really considered and would very much like to hear more about. This, at least, gives the other person the information that they may continue to talk and that you will be interested. Obviously, if you have a reply to make to the question, give it one or two seconds' thought and then present it without being concerned as to whether you are making a good job of your answer. Keep your thoughts orderly and flowing well. This is only a matter of practice and you will have to stumble over your words many times before you become a master of verbal dexterity.

(*iii*) *Telling a story or a joke:* While making small talk it is useful to be able to recount small incidents which have made your own life interesting. The chances are that if they have seemed interesting to you they will to others, although in many cases it is the enthusiasm with which such events are recounted, rather than the events themselves, which makes them enjoyable. If you are to deliver such anecdotes successfully, your best mental strategy is to ensure that you know the key points of the situation or joke around which you can elaborate. Always remember the start, the end and the crucial link phrase of the joke.

(*iv*) *Building up your self-image:* Much of the secret of social and interpersonal success is to have confidence in yourself. But this need not be a product of how much you are able to say, so much as a result of the way in which you can let others know how well you understand their situation. The self-confident person will feel quite at ease, for instance, when listening to others. This behaviour involves reflecting back to the speaker what they have just said in slightly different words so that they feel that you understand their point of view. For instance if they remark that they are irritated at being presented with such a large bill for repairs to their car, the reflective listener might respond with a comment such as: 'Yes, I can see how a bill like that would make you angry.' The unself-confident speaker will often be trying so hard to get a point across that they miss what the other person is saying and come in with a completely inappropriate comment. Practise listening and being an active reinforcer of a speaker. At the end of an encounter where you have been a good reflective listener you will usually find that your partner seems very contented and pleased with the interchange and may even say so. Remember that you can be reflective with body language. 'Aha' with an open-faced nod will encourage the speaker to continue.

3 Crisis tactics

If a social situation is imminent and you have encountered mental or physical barriers in the past, there may not be time to carry out a full behaviour modification programme. Under these circumstances use the following crisis tactics but note that these may also be used, with more practice, as part of a long-term behaviour modification programme.

1 Spend as much time as possible practising relaxation. Carry out several sessions of deep relaxation during the days before the social situation and use quick relaxation at odd moments. Try to use differential relaxation just before and during the social occasion.

2 Try to practise some reflective listening with a friend or relative. Remember that in this skill you are not required to ask any questions or say anything yourself about your own experience. Simply give a rephrased version of what has been said to you, using your own words. Try to show that you understand their feelings.

3 Practise eye-contact in front of a mirror and with a friend or relative when replying to any questions and giving your reflective answer.

4 Practise keeping your breathing regular and relaxed and use natural rest pauses in conversation to regulate your breathing.

4 Long-term behaviour modification

First of all follow the Fourteen-Day Programme in Part Two and when you have familiarised yourself with the principles and skills described begin a Seven-Day Analysis Programme based on your particular social situations and difficulties.

Record keeping
As in the Seven-Day Analysis Programme you will be recording baseline data about your social behaviour under four main headings:

Stimulus – the environment in which the behaviour takes place.
Response – what you did.
Consequence – how you or others reacted to what you did.
'*What I would like to have done*' – your desired behaviour under those circumstances.

See Example Eight.

Structuring a pathway of sub-goals
In Example Eight the following pieces of inappropriate behaviour may be identified:

1 Inability to relax and control anxiety in social situations.
2 Inability to answer when asked for an opinion and expand upon the views.
3 Inability to follow another's conversation effectively.

The major sub-goals in a programme of behaviour modification based on the example might be:

1 Quick and differential relaxation training.
2 Anxiety management training with a friend.
3 Reflective listening training with a friend, using eye-contact and face and head movements.
4 Reflective listening whilst practising differential relaxation and anxiety management.
5 Observation of social behaviour in real life situations.
6 Practising answering questions quickly from a friend.
7 Answering questions quickly with differential relaxation in real life situations.
8 Following conversations using reflective listening combined with asking pertinent questions in real life situations.

Example eight – Typical entry on day one of monitoring

Life area: C – Social and interpersonal relationships

Goal: 'I would like to be able to make new friends easily and confidently'

Behaviour to be monitored: Reponses when meeting people for the first time in social situations.

Stimulus	Response	Consequence	'What I would like to have done'
9.00 p.m. Been at party for ten minutes. Not everyone arrived yet, people standing in groups of three or four drinking and chatting. See one group which looks as though they were having an interesting conversation and would like to join them. Feel tense and not fitting in. Feel will not be able to cope with taxing questions about myself.	Try to think of a way of breaking into group and hover on the outside about three feet away for several minutes. Several points at which I could have said something relevant but felt anxious and tense in case they ignored me.	After a few minutes the group broke up and the members formed other groups from which I was again excluded. Felt disappointed at missing the opportunity.	Stroll over to the group, introduce myself and ask if I could join them right away. This would have given me a place in the group and made it easier to make any comments.

You should practise these skills and strategies using the techniques of self-reinforcement explained in the Fourteen-Day Programme. Of major importance are such reinforcers as mentally congratulating yourself after a period of effective reflective listening and relaxing quickly after a social encounter.

Summary

Social behaviour is not an automatic response with which we come equipped from birth. Each social situation and cultural environment will require a set of social skills special to itself. This means that such skills must be learned over a period of time and practised in order to become efficient.

Important physical and mental skills necessary to overcome the various barriers which may prevent you from effective social behaviour have to be practised at both a verbal and a non-verbal level.

After practising the component skills of social behaviour with an understanding friend, and later in social situations, you will gradually be able to combine the skills into a flexible repertoire of social behaviour.

Goal three – 'I would like to be able to make a formal or informal speech fluently'

The fluent and confident behaviour which we observe in the performance of an experienced and confident speaker often disguises the fact that he or she is carrying out, apparently without effort, a highly skilled piece of behaviour. In reality delivering a speech, whether formal or off-the-cuff, usually requires considerable practice. In developing the ability to present material effectively, the successful public speaker will have acquired several learned skills which are integrated to provide maximum impact in the delivery.

In this goal we shall examine the ways in which barriers to successful public speaking may arise and the strategies by which a confident and effective delivery may be established.

1 Identifying areas of difficulty

In order to identify possible difficulties and areas where physical skills and mental strategies may be lacking from your public speaking behaviour, complete the following ten statements by selecting one, or both, of the alternatives which most closely reflect your own behaviour in a similar situation.

1 During the few days before giving a formal talk
(a) I spend sleepless nights, tense and anxious at the thought of talking. (b) I cannot order my points for presentation in the talk.

2 On the day of the talk
(a) I am unable to eat properly, if at all, because my stomach is churning and I feel sick with anxiety. (b) The thoughts about my subject become more and more confused as I get nearer the talk.

3 As I am being introduced to talk
(a) I sweat, become tense, and feel the room begin to swim.
(b) I keep wondering what people will think about me if I make a mistake or stumble in my delivery.

4 When I begin to talk
(a) I feel my body tremble and panic rise as I feel I am going to lose control. (b) My notes look jumbled and disjointed.

5 Halfway through my talk, whether formal or informal
(a) I feel completely exhausted as though all my energy has been consumed through anxiety. (b) I realise that there is a point which I should have made much earlier to clarify my developing arguments.

6 When I am standing to give a talk
(a) My body feels wooden and my voice sounds monotonous.
(b) I find it very difficult to recapture my train of thought when interrupted.

7 If I am standing in front of an audience to deliver a talk
(a) I either fix my gaze on one person in the audience or avoid all eye-contact completely. (b) I am unable to assess whether my audience is interested or bored.

8 As the time passes during my talk
(a) My speech becomes increasingly rapid and I stumble over the

words. (b) I become more and more concerned about my audience losing interest.

9 If I am asked questions during or after my talk
(a) I become tense and anxious and my colour rises. (b) I become quickly confused and cannot answer the question adequately.

10 If I have to tell jokes during an informal speech
(a) My voice shakes and my body trembles when I rise and during my speech. (b) I find myself taking too long over the joke and losing the pace of telling it.

If you have scored predominantly a's then a major problem of speaking in public is physical tension and anxiety. In this case your behaviour modification programme should include learning relaxation skills and anxiety management so that you can control your level of tension. For further details see under the Physical Skills heading below.

If you have scored predominantly b's then it is likely that a lack of the necessary mental strategies and preparation are resulting in the difficulties. In this case you should practise the skills listed under the Mental Strategies heading below.

A high score in both areas indicates that a combination of mental and physical barriers is arising and preventing you from making speechess effectively. To remove these barriers you should develop programmes which include training in both mental and physical skills.

2 Skills and strategies

Earlier we have indicated that the ability to speak in public must be regarded as a skill which can be learned and practised. Many people attempt to speak in public without any such formal re-hearsal and not surprisingly they run into difficulties.

Physical skills

(*i*) *Relaxation training and anxiety management:* Most people will find that they experience a small amount of anxiety when speaking in public. In small amounts this is often beneficial and may help to key-up their systems sufficiently to give the best performance.

When anxiety becomes acute, however, it may handicap effective delivery and steps must be taken to reduce the level of stress without necessarily removing the arousal completely. The methods of doing this involve quick relaxation training and anxiety management. When acquired this skill enables you to use the potentially disruptive response of anxiety as a beneficial and appropriate response. You can learn to produce a feeling of relaxation and well-being as the consequence of early tension by perfecting three types of relaxation which are detailed in the Fourteen-Day Programme.

1 Deep relaxation will enable you to identify small increases in tension which might, previously, have passed unnoticed.

2 Quick relaxation enables you to settle the autonomic nervous system just before standing up to make a speech or, for example, during the meal after which you know you will have to talk.

3 Differential relaxation is most effective both when you are starting your speech and actually delivering it. It enables you to relax the muscles which are not actually in use and to ease tension in those muscles such as your arms and throat, which are being worked. Such relaxation will prevent trembling, unsteadiness of voice.

When you become experienced in relaxation, perhaps within as little as a week's practice, your body will learn to react to muscle tension by using it as a signal to relax. In this way, tension will be controlled as it occurs.

(*ii*) *Eye-contact – where to look:* For the audience, as well as for the speaker, the most relaxed method of using the eyes is to glance briefly at individual members of the audience from time to time. If you stop to collect your thoughts for a few seconds you might raise your eyes upwards to demonstrate that you are pausing to think. However, when you start again bring your eyes down to meet those of your audience. Avoid the pitfall of singling out one member of the audience to speak to as the others will feel left out. Also, you will begin to feel uncomfortable the longer your eyes stay fixed on that one person. Share your eye-contact time equally between members of your audience.

(*iii*) *Breathing and delivery:* The correct use of pauses when making a speech will make all the difference between a talk which is delivered too swiftly and with too little emphasis to be easily understood and one where the speaker is clearly in control of both his material and his audience. Do not be afraid of pauses and silence, whether for the purpose of drawing a breath, emphasising a point or collecting your thoughts. Take the opportunity at the end of each natural rest pause to take a breath and then to expel it evenly during your next sentence. Maintaining eye-contact with your audience will automatically allow you to expel the words directly at them rather than losing the words above or below the level of their ears. If you find yourself reaching a passage in your delivery where your material has run thin, or where you need respite in order to gather your arguments again use a longer rest pause by incorporating the tactic of asking for questions at that point. This may result in a couple of minutes interchange from members of the audience during which you can be marshalling your facts for the next part of the talk.

(*iv*) *Controlling interruptions:* Although interruptions may be useful for gathering your material together, they can, if extensive, be disruptive to the general flow of your talk. If a particular point of discussion has got out of control or if certain members of the audience keep asking questions to the obvious annoyance of others, it is best to make it clear that while you welcome criticism and discussion of your material it will be to the advantage of all if you can continue your train of thought and deliver your arguments uninterruptedly for a period of time. If you are bringing the audience back from a period of questions which has turned into a general discussion, you may need to raise your voice and announce clearly and precisely that you are about to continue with the main theme of your speech.

(*v*) *Using visual aids:* Another useful method of creating rest pauses in your speech as well as clarifying technical or difficult points for your audience, is to use slides, films, printed notes or, possibly most useful of all, a blackboard. The blackboard is the most flexible of these pieces of equipment since the sensitive speaker can determine from expressions and questions those points which need clarification and amplify those on the board. It also means that you can continue to carry out activities in front of the audience while allowing your voice a rest.

(*vi*) *Body language:* The techniques of stance and facial expression which were described in the previous goal area will also prove useful to the public speaker. These skills can be practised using a mirror.

Mental strategies

(*i*) *How to inspire confidence:* It is of prime importance to demonstrate to your audience from the start that you are in control both of the material and the situation. A hesitant and uncertain opening may make your audience feel ill-at-ease and embarrassed for you. When preparing your notes, ensure that you give yourself instructions for starting the talk, perhaps noting how to address the audience (including the titles, ranks or positions of those present). Then write out your opening remarks in full. Otherwise, except for concluding remarks, your notes should consist of main headings and one or two sub-headings to remind you of important facts and figures during your speech. Never attempt to read a fully written speech as this will sound forced and artificial. Instead, set out your notes so that you are able to deliver your speech flexibly around them and take account of your audience's interest. If they clearly want to hear more about one aspect of your speech, you can shift emphasis slightly. If you are telling anecdotes or jokes, write down your first line, any important link lines and the punch line.

(*ii*) *Length of presentation:* The length of any talk will depend on the expectations of your audience. At a convention or conference you may have to talk for thirty minutes whilst holding the attention of your audience. As guest speaker at a luncheon club your talk may be no longer than ten minutes and include a good deal of anecdotal material. Remember that the most effective speed of delivery will be about one hundred words per minute. Try to ensure that you have the correct amount of material to fit into the time available at this delivery speed.

(iii) Dealing with questions: In stressful situations, where you are faced with good, searching questions with which you have difficulty in coping, you should adopt two major tactics. The first is always to ensure that you have understood the question. When your questioner has finished speaking, say to him or her (and note how close this is to the technique of reflective listening described in the previous goal area) 'I think I understand by your question that you wish me to comment on the following points . . .' then list the points briefly. The second stage, if you feel you need it, is to state that you will think about these points for a few seconds. If you do this and tell your audience so, they will wait patiently while you collect your thoughts since they know what you are doing. If you simply stand or sit there without speaking they may become restive and disrupt you with murmurs or shuffling. If, after considering the points, you are able to answer them all, do so in the most convenient order for you. Discuss the points, possibly using some notes which you have jotted down while you were thinking. If you can answer only one of the points raised, then state that while you have no particular conviction or thoughts on the other points and nothing of value to offer, you would like to expand on the point with which you feel confident. If you are unable to answer any of the points raised do not be afraid to state your position and to ask the questioner or any other member of the audience if they could make a contribution.

3 Crisis tactics

Although we recommend a long-term programme for behavioural modification of serious public speaking difficulties an urgent need to overcome some of the major barriers to success in this area can be eased by use of the following tactics. These may be learned in a couple of days and will be effective in getting you through an imminent public speaking engagement. However, you should then go on and practise the full programme if you wish to be even more effective.

Physical skills
Practise the techniques of relaxation. Carry out deep relaxation

as often as you can and use quick relaxation while preparing your notes and at any other odd moment. Use relaxation before going to sleep and prior to standing up to begin your talk. Practise delivering your talk two or three times in its entirety whilst using differential relaxation. Use a mirror or a couple of friends as your audience.

Mental strategies
There is hardly ever too little time to jot down a few notes before giving a talk. Obviously the notes will be better and of more value to you if you have had longer to prepare them but even fifteen minutes before, for example, the task of replying to a toast at a social function may provide you with enough time to make some quick notes. Always have at least a few lines of notes to guide you and prevent your drying up. Remember to programme in points during your delivery at which to invite your audience to participate. Remember to keep your delivery even and your breathing regular.

4 Long-term behaviour modification

Start by going through the Fourteen-Day Programme outlined in Part Two of this book. Then carry out the Seven-Day Analysis Programme described in Part Three. Since it may be difficult to find a number of real life conditions where you have to perform in public, you should use mock situations using members of your family or friends to help you.

Record keeping
As in the Seven-Day Analysis Programme you will be recording baseline data about your behaviour under four main headings:

Stimulus – the environment in which the behaviour takes place.
Response – what you did.
Consequence – how you or others reacted to what you did.
'*What I would like to have done*' – your desired behaviour under those circumstances.

See Example Nine.

Example nine – Typical entry on day one of monitoring

Life area: C – Social and interpersonal relationships

Goal: 'I would like to be able to make a formal or informal speech fluently'

Behaviour to be monitored: Giving a talk to a small group

Stimulus	Response	Consequence	'What I would like to have done'
3.00 p.m. Seminar starting and group leader announcing me. Feel stomach unsettled. Had no lunch because of anxiety. Look at my notes and see that some of the material is unreadable.	Start to speak and blush. Feel anxiety rise as cannot concentrate on opening sentence. Looking at the paper rather than the audience. Sit solidly in chair and stumble through opening phrases.	Have difficulty in developing the theme of my talk and, when able to glance briefly at the audience notice they seem to be bored.	Stand up and start to speak in such a way that I catch the audience's attention at once and feel confident and in control of my material. Look them in the eyes and project my voice firmly and effectively across the room.

Structuring a pathway of sub-goals

The Seven-Day Analysis will enable you to pin-point both mental and physical barriers which are preventing your success in public speaking. List these inappropriate behaviours clearly. In Example Nine they may be:

1 Inability to relax and control voice trembling.
2 Inability to keep train of thought on topic.
3 Inability to prepare notes to guide the talk.
4 Inability to introduce mobility and voice tone.

The sub-goals towards the overall goal of speaking successfully in public might be arranged as follows:

1 Deep relaxation training.
2 Quick relaxation training.
3 Differential relaxation training while delivering a talk to a friend.
4 Practising writing down notes and link phrases.
5 Practising mannerisms and gestures.
6 Practising eye-contact.
7 Practising voice projection and breath control.
8 Asking for questions and remembering where you were in your talk.
9 Talking informally to a small group, perhaps family or friends.
10 Delivery of speech in a formal situation.

These sub-goals should be practised using self-reinforcement and reinforcement from others, such as the friend with whom you are practising, to increase your performance. Remember that small activities such as taking sips of water during a talk can act as re-inforcers since your mouth will have become dry and the water itself will act as a primary reward.

Ultimately, of course, you will receive reinforcement from the reaction of your audience.

Summary

Speaking effectively in public is a piece of behaviour which must be practised in order for you to become proficient.

To be an interesting and confident public speaker you have to be able to work flexibly from a set of brief notes, take into account the needs of your audience and remain in command of the situation even when stating that you do not have a piece of information which has been requested.

Physical and mental barriers may be overcome by anxiety management, relaxation and strategies of preparation and delivery.

Life area D – Leisure and sport

In this life area we will deal with difficulties and strategies involved in the following commonly expressed goals:
'I would like to be able to . . .

1 fly on holiday or business in a relaxed manner.'
2 play a game of golf while controlling the effects of stress on key strokes.'
3 pass my driving test.'

Goal one – 'I would like to be able to fly on holiday or on business in a relaxed manner'

On looking around on aircraft full of passengers, you will usually see several who seem anxious and unhappy whilst others appear relaxed, at ease and enjoying themselves. If one measured the physical responses of the passengers scientifically there would be several more who, while outwardly controlled, were suffering high levels of tension, heart rate and sweating before and during the flight. The incidence of flight phobia is much more common than most people realise.

Although there are some popular strategies for dealing with the fear of flying, these have such disagreeable and undesirable side effects as the drowsiness and lethargy induced by taking tranquillisers and the debilitating hangover which follows a flight managed only by drinking heavily.

Because of this fear many people, from members of families who make only one return flight a year on their vacation to jet-set executives who may be taking flights each week, find the whole process of journeying a nightmare. For many days before the flight tension and anxiety may mount and spoil what could be a pleasurable anticipation of the journey to come. At the time of the flight, tension may be acute and result in such physical symptoms as headaches, exhaustion, nausea, hypertension and other factors associated with anxiety. After the flight the sufferer may be so exhausted that it takes several days – which may account for the complete length of a short holiday – to recover.

The major components of a fear of flying are those of physical anxiety and lack of mental preparation. In this goal area we shall describe how to develop the necessary physical skills and mental strategies for dealing effectively with flight travel.

1 Identifying areas of difficulty

To help you identify those physical skills and mental strategies which you need to develop in order to fly without fear, complete the following ten statements by selecting one, or both, of the alternatives given which most closely reflect your own behaviour in a similar situation.

1 During the few days before a flight
(a) I have difficulty in sleeping because I become tense and anxious when I think about my journey. (b) I keep telling myself that the journey will be a nightmare.

2 On the morning of the flight
(a) I am unable to eat and my stomach is lurching with anxiety.
(b) I keep trying to think and panicking to find ways out of taking the flight.

3 At the airport
(a) I sweat, feel sick, and very tense. (b) I cannot get my mind off the possible disasters which could take place in the air.

4 When I get into the plane
(a) I sit tensely in my seat with my eyes tightly closed and my fists clenched. (b) I keep looking all the while for the exits.

5 As the plane begins to fill up

(a) I sweat and shake all over. (b) I feel ashamed that I am the only person in the whole plane feeling so anxious.

6 As the aircraft prepares for take-off

(a) I grip my seat and my heart races with anxiety. (b) I feel totally convinced that the plane will crash and that I am going to die.

7 When the plane is in the air and the smallest change, such as a bump, occurs

(a) I jump violently and my anxiety soars. (b) I immediately believe the plane is going out of control.

8 Before and during my flight

(a) I find my muscle co-ordination goes awry. (b) I become confused and cannot answer questions clearly, or find my way around.

9 After the flight

(a) I feel totally exhausted and wet with sweat. (b) I dread the thought of the return trip as disaster must surely occur.

10 If I have work to do during the flight

(a) My hand shakes and I am unable to write clearly. (b) I cannot concentrate my thoughts on my work and am continually wondering if the aircraft is still flying safely.

If you have scored predominantly a's then a major problem in flying is clearly physical tension and anxiety. In this case your behaviour modification programme should include learning relaxation skills and anxiety management so that you can reduce stress to a manageable level. For further details see under the Physical Skills heading.

If you have scored predominantly b's then it looks as if a lack of the necessary mental strategies is producing difficulties. In this case you should practise the skills listed below under the Mental Strategies heading.

A high score in both areas indicates that a combination of mental and physical barriers is arising to prevent you from flying without fear. To remove these barriers you should construct a programme which includes training in both mental and physical skills.

2 Skills and strategies

The ability to fly in a relaxed and confident manner can be learned. The fact that you may now suffer anxiety when flying is due to learning processes which we described earlier in this book. If your responses are mainly those of physical tension and anxiety then your autonomic nervous system has become conditioned to produce sympathetic arousal in the presence of an aircraft or merely at the thought of flying. If you predominantly tell yourself that flying is dangerous and that you cannot cope then you are conditioning your cerebral thoughts and learning an attitude of fearful mental behaviour towards flying.

Physical skills

(*i*) *Relaxation training:* You should devote a good deal of time to developing your relaxation skills. Make sure that you follow the instructions given in the Fourteen-Day Programme, becoming competent in the ability to relax your body quickly and differentially. Although this may take several days, you should not attempt to do anything else at this stage other than gain proficiency in relaxation.

(*ii*) *Anxiety management:* You must learn how to produce your relaxation response whenever stimuli concerning aircraft occur. Remember that the development of an anxiety response is a spiralling action. It starts with the stimulus which produces anxiety, for instance the thought of your journey, getting into the aircraft or taking off. That stimulus leads to a small degree of sympathetic arousal (anxiety). This small level of anxiety, in turn, leads to a higher level of anxiety when you start to become anxious about your anxiety. In turn that greater level of anxiety triggers yet higher levels until, after a few seconds or minutes, you become extremely anxious and panic.

In using anxiety management you must learn to notice the first small surge of anxiety which immediately follows exposure to your feared stimulus – the thought, sight or movement of an aircraft. When you have been able to notice this first surge of anxiety, you should then immediately use quick relaxation. If you regularly make use of quick relaxation in this way you will gradually teach yourself to respond to the first surge of anxiety, not with greater levels of anxiety but with relaxation. Having relaxed quickly, you can carry on to relax even more deeply so that this time your parasympathetic nervous system starts a positive spiral. Instead of growing more and more tense you become increasingly relaxed.

In order to do this effectively, you should practise using rapid anxiety management with those situations related to flying which are not too difficult. If merely thinking about flying causes a small degree of anxiety, use this to produce that first surge of fear and then relax quickly to counteract it. Gradually apply the same technique to situations which you find increasingly fearful until, eventually, you are using it during the actual flight.

After a time you will experience a gradual reduction in the effort needed to switch on your relaxation response. You will find that it becomes quite automatic for you to relax at the thought and reality of a flight instead of becoming tense.

Mental strategies

The attitude which you have developed about air travel will contribute considerably to your learned fear of flying. In many cases, it may be that you are talking yourself into becoming anxious by continually thinking about disasters and the dangers of air travel.

(*i*) *Developing coping statements:* Probably the phrases about flying which you use to yourself and in conversations are of the type: 'I don't know how anyone can fly . . . it fills me with terror', 'I am sure the plane will crash', 'I would rather not go on holiday than fly . . .' and so on. Such statements predispose you to feeling anxious and must be replaced, if you are to fly happily, by more realistic ones.

In learning coping statements we are not suggesting that you should change these statements to ones such as: 'Flying is completely safe and accidents never happen'; 'I shall have no problems whatsoever with my flight'. These statements are as unrealistic as the first ones. Instead, the statements which you develop must be of the type: 'There may be a little difficulty with the journey – delays, bad weather and so forth – but I know that I have the skills to manage anxiety and I shall put them into effect to overcome tension.'

Of great importance are those situations which occur on your first attempts at flying without fear. You must look back on your flight and try to assess what it was you did that made your flight or at least part of it enjoyable. You should then build these memories into your coping statements. For instance: 'I expect that there will be one or two hitches with my next flight, but I know that striking up a conversation with my neighbour was useful last time so there is every reason why it should work again.' In other words, feed into your future flights positive methods of coping gained from past experience.

3 Crisis tactics

If you have a flight in the near future and feel anxious about it we would recommend the following crisis tactics in order to give yourself the best chance of flying in a relaxed way.

Physical skills

Practise all the relaxation skills intensively. While in a relaxed state picture yourself going to the airport, sitting in the departure lounge, walking confidently out to the aircraft and finally taking off without tension. When you actually arrive at the airport spend the time in the departure lounge relaxing quietly. Remain in this relaxed state while boarding the aircraft and during the flight.

Mental strategies

Try to recall some situation in the past, not necessarily to do with flying, which was difficult to manage. Remember how you got through this difficult patch. Now try to develop a coping statement which you can take onto the plane with you which refers to the fact that the plane journey may look as though it will be difficult but that you will be able to cope as in your previous difficult situation. Try to carry that thought with you before and during the plane journey. For example: 'I think the trip may present its difficulties, but I know that I can cope with such difficulties as I did when I had to face my angry boss over trouble at work.'

4 Long-term behaviour modification

In this case, unless you are a regular air traveller with chronic anxiety, carrying out the Fourteen-Day Programme described in

Part Two of this book will be difficult. If your air journeys are frequent use them to produce baseline data. If, however, you travel only infrequently then try to remember occasions on which you flew and use those memories together with your imagination to build up a series of situations which you will know will occur and which you fear.

Record keeping
As in the Seven-Day Analysis Programme you will be recording baseline data about your behaviour under four main headings:

Stimulus – the environment in which the behaviour takes place.
Response – what you did.
Consequence – how you or others reacted to what you did.
'*What I would like to have done*' – your desired behaviour under those circumstances.

See Example Ten.

Structuring a pathway of sub-goals
The analysis will enable you to pin-point those mental and physical barriers which are preventing you from flying happily. List these inappropriate behaviours clearly as those, taken from Example Ten:

1 Inability to relax.
2 Inability to manage anxiety.
3 Inability to develop coping statements concerned with flying.
4 Inability to build up a new attitude to flying.

The sub-goals towards the overall goal of flying in a relaxed and confident manner might be arranged as follows:

1 Deep relaxation training.
2 Quick relaxation training.
3 Differential relaxation training.
4 Developing a hierarchy of situations producing progressively higher levels of anxiety, for example:

(a) Going to travel agent and asking about air flights.
(b) Looking at aircraft brochures.
(c) Visiting an airport to look around.

Example ten – Typical entry on day one of monitoring

Life area: D – Leisure and sport

Goal: 'I would like to be able to fly on holiday or business in a relaxed manner'

Behaviour to be monitored: Responses before, during and after one complete return trip on an aircraft. *

Stimulus	Response	Consequence	'What I would like to have done'
9.35 a.m. In aircraft with seat-belt fastened. Have window seat and two other people on my left. Plane thirty minutes late in leaving due to mechanical trouble. Own tension has been mounting because of delay as well as flight itself. Weather overcast with some light rain.	Tried to close my eyes and block out the thought that I was about to fly. The more I tried the more my heart began to race. Felt sick and had to reach for handkerchief.	Had to drink several large whiskies in order to endure the situation. Could not work on plane as a result of this and my anxiety.	Remained physically calm and concentrated on all aspects of taking off and flying enjoyably. Been able to work on the papers and arrive fresh at the end of my journey.

*Note: Where the piece of behaviour is performed very infrequently as happens here, one trip may well provide sufficient data for monitoring purposes.

(d) Talking to ground staff about their airline.

(e) Watching from the windows as aircraft land, take-off and are refuelled.

(f) Planning a journey.

(g) Preparing breakfast on the morning of the journey.

(h) Travelling to the airport.

(i) Waiting in the departure lounge.

(j) Walking towards the aircraft.

(k) Entering the aircraft.

(l) Finding a seat and settling into it.

(m) The take-off.

(n) The flight, including a bumpy passage.

(o) The landing.

5 Practising each of the items in your hierarchy in imagination while relaxed, reducing your anxiety to each in turn before going on to imagine the next.

6 Carry out the situations in reality while remaining relaxed.

During this programme be sure to end each sub-goal practice session with a reinforcer. After you have planned flight arrangements with your spouse, for instance, you might watch a favourite TV programme together.

Summary

Flying in a relaxed and confident manner is a piece of behaviour which may be learned even though at present flying fills you with dread. To achieve the goal of relaxed flying you should practise the physical skills of relaxation and mental coping strategies and use them first of all in imagination and then in reality.

Goal two – 'I would like to be able to play a game of golf while controlling the effects of stress on key strokes'

It has been rightly said that the most important distance in golf is the nine inches between the golfer's ears, for the development of the correct mental approach to the game is of primary importance. However, it is necessary to break down the mental approach con-

222

cept into various strategies concerned with the swing, the match play, the preparation and tactical decision-making on the course. There is no substitute, ultimately, for professional coaching in golf. But while a good professional can teach you the basic elements of the game, it is seldom that he will then go on to show you how to build up a series of mental strategies which will dramatically enhance your game.

On the physical level, it is necessary to train your muscles not only in the form of your swing and stance but also in a general way to become sufficiently relaxed to accept instruction from the brain effectively. For this reason we shall concentrate on the skills of relaxation training.

1 Identifying areas of difficulty

In order to help you identify which areas in your game are presenting you with difficulties, and to ascertain whether you should concentrate on mental or physical skills, complete the following list of ten statements by choosing one, or both, of the alternatives which most closely reflect your own behaviour in a similar situation.

1 Whenever I think about a match on friendly or competitive terms
(a) I feel tense and nervous. (b) I wonder if my bad strokes will let me down again.

2 Just before stepping out onto the first tee
(a) I feel myself tensing or perspiring. (b) I look around to see whether anyone will be watching me make any blunders.

3 When driving from the tees
(a) I feel inappropriate tension in my arms and legs. (b) I see images of the ball landing in the rough.

4 When my ball lands in a bad lie
(a) I feel physically anxious and become tense. (b) I cannot think of the correct club or tactic to use.

5 After I have played a bad stroke
(a) I also muff the next few strokes because of my tension.

(b) I imagine that I am in for a run of bad luck and tell myself I am going to miss the next few shots.

6 On the greens
(a) I find myself shaking or tense in an uncomfortable position.
(b) I cannot take my time because I feel flustered with other players present.

7 With an aggressive opponent
(a) I find my swing disrupted as I try to alter my game. (b) I keep thinking that he is being critical of me and putting my game down.

8 When in an important match with spectators present
(a) I become physically anxious and tense. (b) My attention is divided between the spectators and my game and I cannot concentrate sufficiently on my strokes.

9 Before a match or before certain holes are played
(a) I fiddle nervously or pace up and down. (b) My mind goes a blank and I cannot think of effective strategies to employ.

10 When trying to improve a swing or trying to get rid of a fault
(a) I become tense if I do not improve rapidly. (b) I get trapped into looking at small details rather than improving my overall appearance.

If you have scored predominantly a's then a major problem in your game appears to be physical tension or anxiety. In this case your behaviour modification programme should include learning relaxation skills so that you can reduce stress to a manageable level and produce a muscular state most likely to result in a successful swing. For further details see under the Physical Skills heading below.

If you have scored predominantly b's then it looks as if you lack the necessary mental strategies to lift your game to a higher level of efficiency. In this case you should practise the skills listed below under the Mental Strategies heading.

A high score in both areas indicates that a combination of mental and physical barriers arises to prevent you from playing at your best. To remove these barriers you should construct a programme which includes training in both mental strategies and physical skills.

2 Skills and strategies

It is obvious that playing a good game of golf must be regarded as a high-level skill which depends, in turn, on a series of sub-skills. Many golfers look upon their game as either 'bad' or 'good' without attempting to break down their overall behaviour into smaller and more manageable parts. Not surprisingly, a person who has come to see his game as a bad one often runs into trouble because he plays as he expects to.

Physical skills

At a physical level there are three important skills which can be learned to improve your game dramatically. These involve muscle training to prevent fatigue, differential muscle relaxation to enable maximum control to be given and anxiety or stress management to remain calm under pressure.

(*i*) *Muscle training:* Any group of muscles which is worked unusually hard without prior training will rapidly become tense, tired and almost certainly suffer from cramp. It will quickly cease to function properly and, particularly in the case of golf, may result in a poor performance after the turn back to the clubhouse. The muscles involved in golf include those in all areas of the body except the face and jaw. For this reason, if you wish to develop your game to a higher level of proficiency, it will be necessary for you to exercise the muscles regularly by following a programme of training, perhaps for only ten minutes each day. You should concentrate not only on building up strength, perhaps by isometric exercises, but also on building up your stamina. It is this second factor which can help you to keep your concentration during the last few holes while your less fit opponent is suffering from fatigue and can only think about the nineteenth hole and collapse into an armchair.

The ability to walk perhaps three or four miles in the course of an hour without undue fatigue is clearly of value. It will certainly be of great value for you to increase your daily walking as shown in the Fourteen-Day Programme.

(*ii*) *Relaxation training:* In sending a complex set of instructions from the brain to the muscles of the body, as during the stance

225

and swing of golf, it is important that the impulses which activate the muscles are as free as possible from any random impulses due to excessive tension. Clearly, if the muscles can be free from non-essential movements and tensions then the precise instructions for them to behave in a certain way will have the maximum chance of being effective.

It is for this reason that the golfer should approach his shots and his overall game while remaining as relaxed as possible. The smooth swing is a product of accurately programming a complex series of muscles. The jerky, and often inaccurate swing is a result of imposing mental commands on an existing high level of muscle tension. Of course, at the time of the swing, and while walking between strokes, certain muscles come under tension. For this reason differential relaxation is a vital skill to learn and to employ on the course. Practice in all the relaxation skills detailed in the Fourteen-Day Programme is necessary to maximise the efficiency of your game.

(iii) *Anxiety management:* Possibly the most daunting moment for most golfers is the tee shot on the first hole. At this point, while your game has yet to reach a complete harmony of muscle and mental balance, you are in full view of others in line for the tee as well as those looking on idly from the clubhouse. If, at this point, you strike the ball badly it may take you several holes to unwind and recover from the humiliation of going a shot or two over on the first hole. At a more advanced level of play, on the day of the club, county or international match or tournament, you may come under stress before even a meagre gathering of spectators. Each time you approach the ball you can feel the hundreds of eyes burning into you as they watch for the slightest hesitation in your swing. In just the same way, the few shots which follow an unfortunate miss-hit can be times at which your autonomic nervous system plays havoc with your muscle control.

In all of these situations you must remember that the development of anxiety follows the form of an ever-widening spiral. It begins with an anxiety producing stimulus, for instance the first tee, the murmur from the crowd or the next swing after a badly sliced shot. Your first sensation will be a small surge of adrenalin into your bloodstream as your stomach lurches slightly. A small degree of tension may also creep into your previously relaxed stride. As you think about this internal feeling it, in turn, becomes a stimulus which produces an even higher degree of anxiety. This spiral, once started, ends with your standing ready for your next shot, perspiring, tense, and panicked by the thought that you must, inevitably fail.

In anxiety management you learn to notice this first, small surge of tension which is the immediate consequence of your feared stimulus. As soon as you feel it you immediately implement your quick and differential relaxation training. As you walk towards the ball, carry out differential relaxation so that the first small feeling of anxiety acts as a trigger for a gradual unwinding of the muscles. Then use this unwinding process as a trigger for further unwinding, until, by the time you are ready to address the ball and take your swing, you are once again relaxed and your muscle system is back under control. In this way, you can use the very necessary warning signal of a small surge of anxiety, which itself means that you are in a situation which needs delicate handling, to lead to progressively greater degrees of relaxation and control over your muscles.

As you practise this in successive games, you will find that you are able to induce rapid anxiety management. First of all you can use it with the less stressful situations and then with those which present most tension, until it becomes quite automatic for you to relax at the thought and realities of approaching your first tee, a difficult lie, or a crucial shot in the game.

Mental strategies

The mental approach to the game of golf has changed considerably in recent years. The days when golfers practised the minutest detail of their backswing for hours on end before allowing themselves to strike a ball are over. They have been replaced by the approach which asserts that given a correct grip, something which a club professional can teach, the correct path of the head of the club will naturally co-ordinate all the component parts of the swing. The mental approach is much more concerned with the blending of the mind and body rather than over-analysis.

(*i*) *Talking to yourself:* In approaching any shot or, indeed, any moment at all in your game, it is essential that you form realistic statements in your mind about the complexity of the shot or your position and the likelihood of a successful outcome. It is necessary to assume at all times that having struck the ball it will arrive at, or near, the point for which it was intended. Try, as you approach and address the ball, to form a mental image of the ball leaving its present position and being projected on to the next intended part of the course.

It is essential that you eliminate from your mind two common errors of thought. The first is to think 'I will just hit it and hope it lands somewhere better.' In this situation you are convincing yourself that good fortune, a notoriously elusive figure, has control over the destiny of your swing. Once you have abdicated responsibility as controller of your strokes you enter a spiral of failure. The second error is that of telling yourself 'Well, there goes the game completely. I might as well give up as I know from past experience that my next few shots will be disastrous.' Here, you are not only surrendering to fate but you are actually predisposing yourself to fail in your shots. Remember that, in general, we do what we expect to do. If you expect to fail on that stroke you will do so.

These failing statements should be replaced by images and statements of a positive nature. Instead of thinking about your proneness to shanking or slicing, concentrate on where you are going to make your ball land. Do not avoid choosing the correct iron for the shot just because you do not like using it. Take it and imagine vividly, especially during a couple of practice swings, your hitting the ball squarely and placing it ideally. Then move to your final address of the ball with that image firmly implanted in your mind's eye. In this way you will stop yourself from over-analysing your stance and swing. If you imagine a successful stroke your swing will automatically fall into place.

One final word on talking positively to yourself. Each shot should be considered independently of any other shot which you play. If, through ill-chance, fatigue or sheer lapse of attention, you miss-hit, even while having approached the ball with the correct mental strategy, never assume that the strategy does not work for you. If you believe that talking yourself into making a good shot will work, then statistically, over a large number of shots, you will find that this expectation is fulfilled. But if you tell yourself you will fail you always will.

(ii) *Swing synthesis:* Once you have developed the basic features of the grip, stance and head position you should avoid all temptation to analyse minute details of your swing which you believe may be causing a problem in your shots. Such analysis will only lead to a gradual deterioration in your overall swing. Consider the following analogy. If, as you are driving your car and negotiating difficult traffic conditions in a town, you begin to try to work out how the wheels turn or how the pistons drive the crank-shaft when you press the accelerator pedal, your actual negotiating of obstacles may deteriorate to the point of collision. Your golf swing works in exactly the same way. Try to consider the overall effect of your swing rather than its component parts and you will develop a much smoother, more effective and relaxed style.

(iii) *Disregard the ball:* You will probably find yourself swinging easily and naturally in practice before the actual shot. But, when you finally address the ball and carry out your swing an important change may occur. Instead of swinging as you did with no ball in the way, you may now attempt to strike at the ball rather than swing through it. In golf, the ball should be considered as something which happens to come in contact with the face of the club-head during the course of the swing. Having placed your feet correctly and addressed your ball, forget that it is there at all and just carry out yet another practice swing. See how much more relaxed and natural this feels and, most importantly of all, how much more frequently you strike the ball correctly.

Obviously there are many other mental strategies. Our object has been to start you thinking about the problems which you encounter in *your* game and give some of the ways in which a fresh mental approach may be beneficial.

3 Crisis tactics

In the event of your having a particularly difficult game in the near future, we suggest the following series of exercises which will give you the best chance of success.

Physical skills

You should concentrate particularly on quick and differential relaxation skills and use them during practice swings before the match. Notice how it feels to relax during the swing and try to implement this in your practice swings during the match.

Mental strategies

Look upon the game as one which will present its own individual difficulties but in which there is logically no reason why you should not play each shot as well as you have ever played. Use mental imagery and mental rehearsal to show yourself, in your mind's eye, how you will play your shots. Try to imagine any difficulties which may arise and how you will overcome them. Make sure you fall back on these rehearsed tactics when you are actually playing in a match.

4 Long-term behaviour modification

First of all carry out the Fourteen-Day Programme described in Part Two and an analysis of your golf game as described in Part Three. We would advise that you use seven separate games to analyse your difficulties before proceeding to a programme of change.

Record keeping

As in the Seven-Day Analysis Programme you will be recording baseline data about your behaviour under four main headings.

Stimulus – the environment in which the behaviour takes place.
Response – what you did.
Consequence – how you or others reacted to what you did.
'What I would like to have done' – your desired behaviour under those circumstances.

See Example Eleven.

Structuring a pathway of sub-goals

Your behavioural analysis will enable you to determine those

Example eleven – Typical entry on day one of monitoring

Life area: D – Leisure and sport

Goal: 'I would like to be able to play a game of golf while controlling the effects of stress on key strokes'

Behaviour to be monitored: Address and swings during game.

Stimulus	Response	Consequence	'What I would like to have done'
Approaching the first tee. 10.00 a.m. Line of eight players waiting. Remember the first tee shot last time badly sliced. Feel anxiety rising in case I make a fool of myself. Unable to imagine where the ball will land.	Anxiety increases. Muscles become tense and I am conscious of tension on backswing. Knees tremble and mind blanks. Swing and slice ball badly as go off balance.	Feel humiliated, and convinced that I will play this hole disastrously. Unable to get thoughts back under control.	Approached the tee while concentrating exclusively on this swing. Forgotten previous blunders. Had five or six practice swings imagining the spot where ball would land. Then moved to address and relaxed. Hit ball evenly through relaxed swing.

mental and physical barriers which are preventing you from playing at your best. List your inappropriate behaviours as in Example Eleven:

1 Inability to relax during the address and swing.
2 Inability to keep anxiety at a manageable level.
3 Inability to co-ordinate thoughts about the placing of the ball.

The sub-goals towards the overall goal of playing a game of golf while controlling the effects of stress might be arranged as follows:

1 Deep, quick and differential relaxation.
2 Differential relaxation training during practice swing.
3 Differential relaxation training during practice while spectators look on.
4 Differential relaxation training during the course of a game with one partner.
5 Differential relaxation training during a fourball.
6 Development of mental imagery about the placing of the ball during the address.
7 Consistency in moving towards each shot while working out a positive tactic and mental image.
8 Using differential relaxation and mental imagery during a match with spectators present.
9 Walking from the clubhouse to first tee and playing opening shots with spectators present.

During this programme you should be sure to end each sub-goal by rewarding yourself mentally with praise or tangibly with some activity you enjoy. Continue to keep detailed records for several games but this time write down when and why you performed well. Then use these positive tactics as further mental strategies during your next game.

Summary

Playing a consistently good game of golf is a piece of highly skilled behaviour. To achieve such consistency it is necessary to break the overall skill into sub-skills. Having done this it is necessary to adopt an overall approach to the game so that you always keep the immediate objective and the way in which it can be achieved in mind.

Goal three – 'I would like to be able to pass my driving test'

Driving, like playing a sport, holding a conversation and any other complex activity is known, in behavioural language as an 'open skill'. This distinguishes it from 'closed skills' such as carrying out a set piece of behaviour on the production line, operating a machine or marching in military drill. An open skill is one in which a set of flexible behaviour patterns can be integrated in a wide variety of ways to enable appropriate action to be taken. In driving, there is no set pattern which can be learned to travel along a certain route. It has to be done using a second by second monitoring of conditions and responding to these immediately and flexibly.

When learning to drive we acquire a series of special skills, such as moving the gear shift, turning the steering wheel, looking in the rear-view mirror, signalling, checking the oncoming traffic while overtaking and a variety of associated behaviours which evolve to a state where they can be carried out, without conscious thought, in complex permutations.

The problems which many people encounter when learning to drive, and of course when carrying out their driving test, are those of physical tension and anxiety, especially in relation to certain manœuvres, and mental confusion in co-ordinating various sub-skills into an overall effective handling of the car.

1 Identifying areas of difficulty

In order to help you identify those physical skills and mental strategies which may be lacking from your car driving behaviour, complete the following ten statements by selecting one, or both, of the alternatives given which most closely reflects your own behaviour in a similar situation.

1 On the day of a driving lesson
(a) I become tense and anxious at the thought of driving.

(b) I cannot seem to remember what I have learned on the previous lessons.

2 When driving in traffic
(a) I become afraid that other cars will force me to alter course.
(b) I cannot take in all the signs and signals which I encounter.

3 When overtaking
(a) I become nervous and clutch the wheel tensely. (b) I cannot make up my mind whether or not to pull out.

4 If another motorist cuts in front of me unexpectedly
(a) I become furious inside and frustrated that I cannot get back at him. (b) All my attention is taken from the driving situation and focused on his car.

5 If I try to learn about traffic signs and the theoretical side of driving
(a) My eyes blur as I read the manuals and I become drowsy.
(b) I find I cannot remember the material from one day to the next.

6 As my driving test draws near
(a) I grow very anxious and have sleepless nights. (b) I seem to be able to take in less and less information.

7 On the day of my driving test
(a) I become totally distraught and so nervous that I jump at anything. (b) I am unable to concentrate on driving or take in instruction.

8 When my driving test starts
(a) I am so nervous that I tremble with tension. (b) I keep imagining myself failing especially on the more difficult manœuvres.

9 During my test
(a) My muscles are taut as I wait for the next instruction.
(b) I have to keep asking for instructions to be repeated.

10 If I encounter a difficulty during my test
(a) I find it almost impossible to make my body respond and continue the test. (b) I convince myself that I have failed and give up trying.

If you have scored predominantly a's it looks as though a major problem in passing your test is physical tension and anxiety. In this case your behaviour modification programme should include learning relaxation skills detailed under the Physical skills heading below, so that you can reduce stress to a manageable level.

If you have scored predominantly b's then you seem to lack the necessary mental strategies in your driving. To overcome these difficulties you should practise the skills listed below under the Mental strategies heading.

A high score in both areas indicates that both mental and physical barriers are combining to prevent you from passing your test. To remove these barriers you should construct a programme which includes training in both mental and physical skills.

2 Skills and strategies

Taking a driving test without having learned the sub-skills of driving is inviting failure. For this reason we shall list some basic skills and strategies which will help you in establishing these behaviours and performing them under pressure.

Physical skills
At a physical level there are two very important skills to be learned in order to keep anxiety under control during your period of learning to drive and taking your test.

(*i*) *Relaxation skills:* In all tasks where you have to monitor equipment continuously and carefully, excessive muscle tension can result in jerky, irregular and coarse movement. In order to master the controls and operate them effectively we suggest that you use relaxation methods which are described in the Fourteen-Day Programme in Part Two of this book. When learning quick and differential relaxation methods you should actually sit in the driver's seat of a stationary car and practise moving the wheel, pressing the foot pedals and shifting the gear lever while remaining relaxed. Concentrate especially on your shoulders, arms and face. Keep these relaxed as they are the most common areas of tension in driving.

(ii) Anxiety management: It is very useful when driving to have a small degree of physical arousal as this can serve to key up the system and focus attention. However, after only a small increase in this ideal level, the arousal will start to have a destructive effect on performance and the skills will begin to deteriorate.

It is this phenomenon which you may be experiencing when you attempt to carry out certain driving manœuvres and encounter difficulties. If you have come to associate a certain manœuvre with tension and anxiety, this may build up as you anticipate having to carry out the operation. When actually performing the task, the anxiety spirals until you are sweating, have a pounding heart and tense muscles as you wrestle to make the car perform properly.

In anxiety management, small degrees of productive anxiety arousal may be used as triggers by which to tell yourself to switch in the differential relaxation technique. When you think about carrying out a task you find especially difficult or when you attempt to perform it, notice the first surge of anxiety in your stomach and muscles. Learn to use this, before it spirals out of control, as the trigger for the response of quick and differential relaxation. Having controlled the build-up of anxiety, continue to increase your level of relaxation.

In this way a small amount of anxiety can be used productively to key you up and keep you attentive while also triggering productive relaxation responses. You should try to carry out these anxiety management exercises in your car, preferably in the driving seat, and also when being driven. Even when watching other people driving you can associate quick relaxation with difficult situations. Bring yourself under stimulus control of the car and motoring situations in general so that you can produce the response of relaxation quickly and easily.

Mental strategies

(i) Learning your lessons: If you find that each time you have a driving lesson you have to spend part of it going back over work covered the week before, then you are carrying out passive as opposed to active learning.

Passive learning means simply being taken through a series of procedures whilst letting the instructor make all the decisions.

This type of learning is very unlikely to stay in the memory for longer than a few seconds after it has been carried out. In this case the learning is negligible. Active learning, as the name implies, means taking an active part in the lesson. It means not merely following the instructions but asking yourself frequently why you are performing some particular action. In other words, ask yourself whether you understand the reasoning behind your lesson. Afterwards, go back over the lesson for a few minutes in your mind and make notes about what you did, how you did it and why you did it. In this way, the information will be much more likely to remain in your memory for the next time. You will have associated what you did with reasons which are easily understandable to you and therefore, when you are next in the practical situation, you will have the behaviour ready.

(*ii*) *Procedures for individual manœuvres:* In carrying out manœuvres such as turning, reversing, hill starts and so on you should remember accurately, by active learning, each stage of the operation and how it links to the next stage. You should remember different combinations of traffic and road situations and at what point you operate the pedals or turn the wheel. Before actually carrying out the manœuvre you should run through the sequence in your mind to rehearse the behaviour. Imagine all the component parts in detail and relate them to this situation specifically. Such mental rehearsal need only take a few seconds and you can carry it out whether you are undergoing driving lessons or your driving test. Remember that it is much better to pause for thought than to move too quickly and erratically.

(*iii*) *Motivation under pressure:* If you experience difficulties or situations where someone acts dangerously be ready with a strategy which will enable you to remain in control. The best way of doing this is to develop a series of statements which you can bring to mind immediately a difficult situation arrives. For example you might think to yourself: 'I stalled the car, but I know that if I shift into neutral, use my handbrake and restart it that I shall be able to move off in the normal way' or 'That driver made me brake hard but I shall immediately begin to concentrate once again on the road ahead and not let it distract me'. You must develop these

statements in quite a formal way so that you are ready with a prepared, set line to bring to mind when the occasion arises. It is no
use, when things go wrong, trying to think of some positive statement with no prior thought as this may confuse you even more.
Write down your statements by looking back over the lesson and
noting down what happened to alarm or irritate you. Note down
too what you would have liked to have thought when this happened. This can be done when you are carrying out the Seven-Day
Analysis Programme.

3 Crisis tactics

Although we do not recommend short-term stratagems as the best
method of passing your test, there are some essential skills which
will help you, especially if you are becoming very anxious and
upset about driving. They may also be of great help if your test is
imminent.

Physical skills
Quick relaxation and anxiety management, if practised intensively
for a few days, can produce a startling improvement in your ability
to stay calm and in your attitude to driving. Use these especially
before a lesson or test.

Mental strategies
Try particularly to develop a series of statements which you can
use under stress. Talk to yourself and tell yourself how you are
going to overcome those situations which are likely to arise while
driving. If you have time you should write down and study these
tactics.

4 Long-term behaviour modification

You should first carry out the Fourteen-Day Programme described
in Part Two and the Analysis Programme detailed in Part Three.
Gather baseline data on your present driving ability and think
particularly carefully when you come to write down 'What I would
like to have done'. These notes can provide you with the basis of
your mental coping statements.

Record keeping

As in the Seven-Day Analysis Programme you will be recording baseline data about your driving behaviour under four main headings:

Stimulus – the environment in which the behaviour takes place.
Response – what you did.
Consequence – how you or others reacted to what you did.
'*What I would like to have done*' – your desired behaviour under those circumstances.

See Example Twelve.

Structuring a pathway of sub-goals

Your analysis will enable you to pinpoint mental and physical barriers which are preventing progress in learning to drive and in passing your test. You should list these inappropriate behaviours as in the following example:

1 Inability to relax and control anxiety.
2 Inability to remember instructions from lesson to lesson.
3 Inability to take in instructions given during driving.

The sub-goals towards the overall goal of passing your test might be arranged as follows:

1 Relaxation training.
2 Anxiety management, and quick relaxation in the car.
3 Active learning during and after the lesson.
4 Developing positive statements for difficult situations.
5 Listening actively to instructions in the car by repeating them immediately in your mind.
6 Practising a driving test situation with your instructor or a friend.
7 Using relaxation skills and coping sentences during the driving test.

At all points in practising these sub-goals you must take care to use effective reinforcement involving both praise and material rewards such as a cigarette, cup of coffee and so on. Remember that it is essential to follow the piece of behaviour immediately with the reward.

Example twelve – Typical entry on day one of monitoring

Life area: D – Leisure and sport

Goal: 'I would like to be able to pass my driving test'

Behaviour to be monitored: Behaviour during driving lessons

Stimulus	Response	Consequence	'What I would like to have done'
In car with instructor in town with heavy traffic. Raining slightly. Daylight going. Feeling apprehensive as this is the first time in dusk driving. Car cuts across from outside lane causing me to brake suddenly.	Surge of fear. Stomach turns over. Grip wheel tightly and slam foot to pedal. Car skids slightly. Afterwards begin to tremble and shake and tell the instructor that I cannot continue.	Instructor tells me that I have been told how to cope with such a situation and that I had over-reacted badly. I am still unable to continue and the instructor takes us back.	Reacted quickly but less fiercely then told myself to regain control of the steering and proceeded slowly watching that the car did not disturb my rhythm again. Focused attention quickly on to the traffic conditions ahead.

Summary

Learning to drive and pass the test is an open skill which may be practised and learned by developing the component skills. To be effective you have to develop physical and mental skills and strategies relevant to managing anxiety and learning to cope in changing situations and these must be practised regularly.

Taking and passing your test requires using a flexible combination of the component skills while under external pressure from the examination situation and this should be practised under mock conditions.

Part six

How to sustain the habit of success

How to sustain the habit of success

The purpose of this book has been to show you that there is nothing mystical or impossible about achieving success in any area of life you choose. As you will now realise, attaining fulfilment of your goals depends initially on being able to state those goals in a realistic and attainable way and then performing the appropriate behaviour necessary to achieve them.

Appropriate behaviours include being able to structure a pathway of sub-goals which you can use as stepping stones towards the overall goal, and maintaining control of your mind and body as you work towards success.

Inappropriate behaviours, as we have shown, fall into two categories. Inappropriate mental processes, where the mind becomes confused and takes the wrong decisions; and inappropriate physical responses, where the autonomic nervous system takes control producing anxiety symptoms which seriously interfere with the performance of the desired behaviour.

Frequently both these responses are present and a spiralling of inappropriate behaviour occurs due to feedback. The mind becomes confused by bodily tension, the physical anxiety increases as mental uncertainty rises.

We have also explained that these incorrect responses to a situation arise because we have learned to behave in that particular way. But just as inappropriate responses have been programmed into the system, correct, goal achieving behaviours can also be learned. Such learning requires only a little time, patience and the correct technique to be effective. If you carry out the programme described in this book you will rapidly replace inappropriate behaviours with appropriate, achieving responses in any area of life you desire.

By using the method of reinforcers, rewarding yourself immediately after you have performed an appropriate piece of behaviour and attained a sub-goal, you will be able to sustain strong motivation for change during the learning period.

Once you have got into the habit of success you will probably wonder why on earth difficulties, which may have seemed insurmountable only a few weeks earlier, ever presented any challenge at all.

We have designed our programmes, on the basis of clinical and practical experience, so as to ensure a smooth and easy transition from your present situation to your desired goals. However, the ways in which information is integrated by the mind and body and the processes by which we learn new skills and behaviours are extremely complex. In order to prevent minor, and inevitable, setbacks from discouraging you during the period of behaviour modification we want to deal finally, and briefly, with the *laws of learning*.

The method by which the human brain absorbs information has been the subject of intense scientific research in the past few decades and we now know a great deal about the different stages of learning through which we pass when mastering a new subject. It is not, as one might suppose, a smooth transition from ignorance to full knowledge, with every effort to learn being equally rewarded. There is no ladder to knowledge, with every hour spent studying a subject being represented by equally spaced steps to the top. Rather, the pathway to understanding a new topic follows the line of the graph in Figure One. The diagram represents the six stages of learning. By going through the Fourteen-Day Programme you have already travelled along the line of the graph in acquiring, even if only temporarily, a new piece of behaviour.

The laws of learning are as follows:

1 Acquisition
2 Plateaux and scalloping
3 Generalisation
4 Internalisation
5 Extinction
6 Recovery

All learning follows this logical sequence.

1 Acquisition

You want to acquire a new set of skills: to speak French, play a

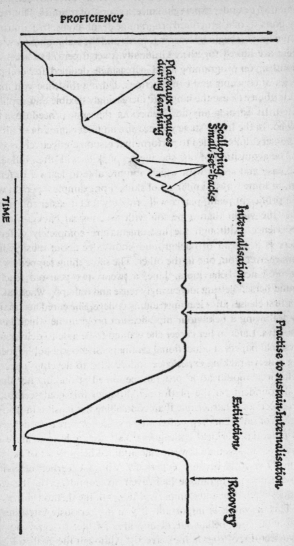

Figure 1

The laws of learning: how we acquire knowledge

PROFICIENCY

TIME

Plateaux – pauses
during learning

Scalloping
Small set-backs

Internalisation

Practise to sustain Internalisation

Extinction

Recovery

sport or learn a profession or trade. To do this you follow, either on your own or under expert guidance, a course of training. This training consists of a structured programme of sub-goals. In acquiring a language you begin by learning words and the techniques by which these are linked together. Gradually, over a period of weeks or months, you programme in an increasingly detailed and complex series of concepts and constructions. During this time you make your ability to use the language increasingly flexible and sophisticated. In learning any new behaviour the same procedure is followed. In the initial stage you acquire an understanding of all the necessary skills needed to perform that response effectively.

The acquisition of one specific set of skills will often influence the ease and speed with which you are able to learn a different yet, in some ways, similar set of skills. For example a person who is a proficient piano player will probably find it easier to learn to play the violin than a person with no musical background or experience. Although the instruments are completely different there is a spread of background knowledge about music which carries over from one to the other. The same thing happens when learning new behaviours. Jane, a twenty-two-year-old teacher, found herself getting increasingly tense and unhappy when taking her first classes after leaving training college. She cured her anxiety by following a behaviour modification programme which lasted ten days. Later in her career she wanted to be able to deliver professional papers at educational seminars. She found public speaking a nerve-racking experience and decided to develop a second behaviour modification programme aimed at making her fluent and confident on the platform. Although this goal seemed, in prospect, a far harder one than controlling her tension in front of a class of small children – after all the speeches were to be delivered to potentially critical colleagues – Jane was able to achieve her new goal in less than a week. She attained her new set of skills as quickly as this because experience with the earlier behaviour modification programme had given her confidence in the techniques of change and familiarised her with the methods involved.

This is why it is important, if you are seriously interested in changing your behaviour in any area of life, to carry out the Fourteen-Day Programme correctly. Although the goals we have selected may seem trivial to you, the fact that you have been able to modify your behaviour even in the small ways suggested will give you confidence when tackling a more complex programme of change. What is more, the familiarity with the methods gained during the Fourteen-Days will stand you in good stead during the later programmes.

2 Plateaux and scalloping

As you go through a behaviour change programme you may notice that there are times when you seem to be making next to no progress towards your chosen sub-goal. Indeed, you may even seem to take a step backwards on some occasions. Do not worry or give up in despair. This is perfectly normal and natural. All it means is that you have arrived at one of the learning plateaux, or dropped into one of the small, scalloped troughs, which crop up on the road to fulfilment. We can liken these flat periods and small troughs to moments of rest or short detours during a stiff, uphill climb. After a period of effort it is pleasant and valuable for the muscles to be able to relax and regain their strength for the next burst of activity. Or sometimes, when too difficult a route has been chosen, the path has to be retraced to find an easier one. Although learning a new piece of behaviour is a great deal less exhausting than climbing a mountain, the mind needs plateaux to consolidate what has been learned and let the new skills sink in. Do not look on such plateaux as a period of wasteful inactivity. Although dramatic changes may not be taking place externally, the mechanisms of learning are making vital use of the plateaux to establish the new behaviours firmly. Do not panic, lose confidence in yourself and the programme or try to force the pace. Keep on with your work towards the next sub-goals and be certain that you are using the techniques of reinforcement to sustain motivation towards the overall goal. Similarly, when you find a small trough in behaviour acquisition, keep working steadily back up the slope again.

Very often, when a plateaux has been reached, you may go through a period of thinking that you have attained an important sub-goal and it would be nice to rest for a moment, or that if you try and pass on to the next goal you may become confused and lose what you have already acquired.

If you do feel tired, then it is perfectly alright to take time off from the programme for a short while. But you must not let these rest periods go on for too long because, as we explained earlier in the book, behaviour which is not practised gets increasingly harder to carry out.

When you have reached your overall goal you will arrive at a major and lengthy plateau. At this point in the learning process, continued practice is still essential because it will help to consolidate the new behaviour and enable you to carry it out with less and less effort and conscious attention.

3 Generalisation

This occurs during the first two periods of learning, the acquisition and plateau stages. During this time you will find that, alongside the main change towards which you are working, other, smaller, changes will be taking place. For example, one man, carrying out a behaviour modification programme to help him get on better with his children at home found, to his astonishment, that his relationships with colleagues at work were also improving. A woman who used a programme aimed at helping her enjoy a more satisfactory sexual relationship with her husband was equally surprised to discover, a few weeks into the programme, that her relationship with her parents was also getting better.

Although you may find this spread of change from the specific area of behaviour modification to other life areas unexpected, it is perfectly logical and obeys the law of learning known as Generalisation. Generalisation occurs in two ways. There is stimulus generalisation and response generalisation.

In stimulus generalisation, learning to behave in a certain way under specific stimulus situations can lead to your behaving in a more appropriate way under different conditions. For example a businessman with ulcers and a heart condition was warned by his doctor that the stress to which he subjected himself while driving might prove fatal. This man was an aggressive and quick-tempered individual who used to take grave exception to the behaviour of other road users. In heavy traffic he would fume and boil, hurling abuse at any other driver who, he believed, had tried to carve him up on the road. He constructed a programme of behaviour change designed to operate in the specific environment of the car. The programme was aimed at curbing the response of anger generated by the stimulus control of the surroundings of a motor car. But he soon found that it was helping him to stay cool and calm under a wide variety of situations which had previously upset him, from business meetings to domestic rows. As a result his whole life became more tranquil and pleasant.

The second type of generalisation is in the area of response. One man developed a programme designed to help him demonstrate emotions to his wife. As he progressed he found, quite unexpectedly, that he was able also to plan and discuss factual issues with her, such as their forthcoming holiday and his business worries without the previously inevitable rows. He also found that he was responding to her much more sympathetically and agreeably in social situations. At the same time his sexual relationship with his wife became easier and more intense. He had experienced the phenomenon of response generalisation during his learning programme.

4 Internalisation

When somebody can carry out a piece of behaviour easily, without conscious effort, they speak of being able to do it 'naturally' or 'instinctively'. We use this to describe the way we speak a language, read and write and perform such complex learned behaviours as driving, playing a sport or making friends. In learning terms we say that the behaviour has been 'internalised'. Most of the things we do in life are internalised skills. When carrying out a behaviour change programme, therefore, it is necessary to look at the learning process as a continuing one which carries on after you have reached the overall goal. It is a mistake to achieve your desired goal and then immediately cease to practise the behaviour, since it will certainly decline with lack of use. Once your overall goal has been reached consolidate it by continued effort. At this point it will become internalised and you may come to look on it as something which is a 'natural' part of your personality.

5 Extinction

Above we said that if we neglect to practise a piece of behaviour it will decline. Eventually it is likely to disappear completely from the behaviour repertoire. This disappearance is known as extinction. Some pieces of behaviour are very resistant to extinction. For example, once you have learned to ride a bicycle or swim you can usually do so immediately even though you have not been near a cycle or water for years. Other behaviours extinguish more rapidly. We may have learned a part in a play or a piece of poetry by heart as a child yet be quite unable to recall more than a few words five years later. We may have learned dancing or playing the piano at school yet be quite incapable of doing either, instantly, within a few years of stopping practising. The only way to avoid extinction of a skill is to practise regularly.

However, although a piece of behaviour may diminish through disuse, nothing which has been learned is ever completely forgotten. Once the chemical and neuronal pathway has been formed in the mind it remains there until death and decay erase the circuits forever. What happens is that, like any pathway, it becomes overgrown. After a time hardly a trace of the route may remain, although it can still be uncovered given a short period of time to clear the accumulated tangle of neglect. The same is true about the old behaviours supplanted by new ones during a programme of behaviour change. They do not vanish forever, they are merely replaced with fresh and more appropriate behaviours. At any time we choose we can return to our old ways should we ever want to do so.

6 Recovery

If you learn a language and then fail to speak it for years, your ability will diminish through extinction as we explained above. But if, perhaps years later, you want to take up that language again, a short course of retraining will re-establish the ability with far less effort than it took to master the language in the first place.

This is known as recovery and applies to every learned piece of behaviour.

As we have said behaviour which has been extinguished is never completely removed from the pathways of the brain, which is why it may be recovered swiftly. If you have not carried out a piece of behaviour for a long period, then brief exposure to a period of practice may bring your behaviour back to full and complete efficiency within a space of time far shorter than your original acquisition period.

So if you have allowed your behaviour modification programme to become disused for a time, perhaps because of a period of ill-health or similar difficulties beyond your control, do not assume that you will have to repeat the entire programme. Instead, take short-term action involving practice of your ultimate goal, or possibly the one or two sub-goals before it, and you should soon find yourself functioning at full efficiency.

Culturally and educationally we are taught, throughout life, to think of our own behaviour as something either inherited and unchangeable or founded in the deep and unfathomable unconscious. In the first case we could be excused for believing that nothing short of brain surgery, electric shock treatment or drugs could have any effect on the way we behave. In the second case we might see no alternative to an extensive and expensive period on the psycho-analyst's couch.

It is hardly surprising that such myths have been perpetuated since they justify the existence of legions of highly-paid professionals and entrepreneurs from psycho-analysts and psychiatrists to drug manufacturers. There are, of course, circumstances in which drugs are essential and medicine performs a valuable function. But to use these as the only, or even the primary, agencies for change is needlessly to abdicate ultimate authority over the two most important and precious rights we possess. An understanding of our behaviour and a control over our future.

Dr Jack Birnbaum
How to Stop Hating and Start Loving 70p

Based on the principles of Transactional Analysis and Gestalt
Therapy, Dr Birnbaum's excellent book shows how anger –
expressed or suppressed, in the right way and at the right time – can
become therapeutic : you are free again to feel affection and joy.
You can stop hating and start loving !

Harry Lorayne
How to Develop
a Super-Power Memory 75p

The author has been described as the man with the most
phenomenal memory in the world . . . Now you, too, can train your
memory to the point where you will never forget names, faces,
numbers, facts, ideas . . . Learn how to remember dates, telephone
numbers, appointments ; greet people instantly by name ; grasp the
ideas expressed in talks, lectures, books – quickly, retaining them
indefinitely ; learn a foreign language in a third of the usual time.

'There is no such thing as a poor memory, only a trained and
untrained one' THE AUTHOR

Mildred Nemman & Bernard Berkowitz
How to be Your Own Best Friend 35p

This remarkable book, written with warmth, understanding and
wisdom, provides simple guidelines to help you become the person
it is in you to be.

'There is no pill made that is as simple, effective and fast-working . . .
positively inspirational' NEIL SIMON

Thomas A. Harris
I'm OK, You're OK 75p

This practical guide to Transactional Analysis is a unique approach to your problems. Hundreds of thousands of people have found this phenomenal breakthrough in psychotherapy a turning-point in their lives.

In sensible, non-technical language Thomas Harris explains how to gain control of yourself, your relationships and your future – *no matter what has happened in the past.*

Lawrence J. Peter & Raymond Hull
The Peter Principle 60p

'For anybody who has ever worked in or (God rest his soul) been head of a big private or public organization, this devilish little book will provide unending material for uneasy reflection' SUNDAY TIMES

'A novel explanation of the incompetence around us ... the book effervesces with anecdotes' THE LISTENER

'There is much to admire in this chain of reasoning and it cannot be denied Dr Peter has made some significant discoveries' THE SPECTATOR

Dr Max Luscher & Ian Scott
The Luscher Colour Test

'You may not agree with what Luscher says, but try asking your friends if they think he's right about you ! Then, try the test on them !' DAILY MIRROR

Dr Max Luscher, Professor of Psychology at Basle University, bases his personality test on the theory that a person's preference for certain colours is directly related to the 'emotional value' of these colours. The colours people prefer, dislike or are indifferent to, are indicators of basic personality traits ...

Harry Maddox
How To Study 60p

Successful study depends not only on ability and industry but on effective methods of working. This invaluable and comprehensive handbook tells you how to obtain the greatest benefit from your studies for the least expenditure of energy and effort. Using the author's methods you can speed up your reading rate, better your ability to memorize and take accurate notes, improve your written English and understand elementary mathematics. Wherever you may be studying, the author will help you to work without supervision and realize your full potential.

G. H. Vallins
Good English 60p

Words 'have enabled us to rise above the brutes and often sink to the level of the demons' ALDOUS HUXLEY

Can you always write exactly what you mean? Are you sometimes at a loss for the right word?

G. H. Vallins states clearly and simply the main principles of current English usage, outlines the basic conventions, and deals entertainingly with jargon, idiom and cliché. It is a perfect guide on how to achieve a good simple style for business and everyday usage.